M000074056

unwanted wisdom

Sheila's Cross
Photo by Billy Winters

unwanted wisdom

Suffering, the Cross, and Hope

Paul G. Crowley, S.J.

continuum

NEW YORK • LONDON

2005

The Continuum International Publishing Group Inc
15 East 26 Street, New York, NY 10010

The Continuum International Publishing Group Ltd
The Tower Building, 11 York Road, London SE1 7NX

Copyright © 2005 by Paul Crowley

Parts of this book are revisions of the following earlier writings: "Between Earth and Heaven: Ignatian Imagination and the Aesthetics of Liberation," in *Through a Glass Darkly: Essays in the Religious Imagination,* ed. John C. Hawley (New York: Fordham University Press, 1996), 50–69; "Rahner's Christian Pessimism: A Response to the Sorrow of AIDS," *Theological Studies* 58 (1997): 286–307; "Homosexuality and the Counsel of the Cross," *Theological Studies* 65 (2004): 500–529.

Cover photo: Unterlinden Museum

All rights reserved. No part of this book may be reproduced, stored in a retrieval system, or transmitted, in any form or by any means, electronic, mechanical, photocopying, recording, or otherwise, without the written permission of publisher.

Printed in the United States of America

Library of Congress Cataloging-in-Publication Data
Crowley, Paul G.
    Unwanted wisdom : suffering, the cross, and hope / by Paul G. Crowley.
      p. cm.
    Includes bibliographical references and index.
    ISBN-13: 978-0-8264-1759-6 (13-digit hardcover : alk. paper)
    ISBN-10: 0-8264-1759-0 (hardcover : alk. paper)
      1. Jesus Christ – Crucifixion. 2. Pain – Religious aspects – Christianity.
    3. Suffering – Religious aspects – Christianity. 4. Hope – Religious
    aspects – Christianity. I. Title.
    BT453.C76 2005
    231′.8 – dc22
                                                                    2005019631

You will stretch out your hands,
and someone will bind you
and lead you where you do not want to go.
(John 21:18)

To Sheila
(1946–1993)

The Almighty has done great things for me.
Holy is His name
(Luke 1:9)

and David
(1959–1994)

You are precious in my sight, you are honored.
And I love you.
(Isa. 43:4)

Contents

Contents

Preface

Zeus, who guided men to think,
. . . has laid it down that wisdom
comes alone through suffering.
Still there drips in sleep against the heart
grief of memory; against
our pleasure we are temperate.
From the gods who sit in grandeur
grace comes somehow violent.

— Aeschylus, "Agamemnon," First Choral Ode[1]

THIS BOOK addresses a conundrum for Christian faith. On the one hand, as Aeschylus said so well, the encounter with suffering forces upon us a wisdom which few would ever ask to receive in so painful and wrenching a fashion. Even worse, we must face the fact that in the midst of suffering and its aftermath, the once familiar landscapes of faith take on unfamiliar and even threatening aspects. Yet the Christian imagination holds out as a symbol of hope the cross of Jesus Christ — on the face of it a most unpromising image if we are looking for a sense of the presence of God in the midst of sufferings that often enough grow to tragic proportions.

In the face of the darkness of suffering, the tendency of some Christians is to place the cross, and all that it stands for, in question: to let a sense of the tragic, the irreversibility of suffering, cast into doubt everything we hold dear. But this is, in a sense, to invert the proper order of things. For we might more profitably read or interpret our suffering in light of the cross, if the cross stands not as a sign of submission to what cannot be changed, but rather as the answer to the questions raised by the sheer darkness of suffering itself. The philosopher Jerome Miller, whose work figures later in this book, puts the "Answer" first in approaching those existential crises that attend the visitations of suffering:

> It is possible to interpret all possible Answers in terms of what a crisis is, instead of interpreting what a crisis is in terms of one of the Answers whose effect is purportedly to end it. Instead of allowing an Answer to govern our understanding of crisis, it is possible to allow our understanding of crisis to govern our evaluation of all possible Answers.... [T]he truth about crisis is a truth every claim to wisdom must integrate, if it is to be congruous with the basic nature of human existence.[2]

This book proposes to understand the cross as the Answer which can govern our understanding of suffering. But it is suffering itself that must, in turn, inform any understanding of the cross, and for this reason, the book begins with an attempt to describe, or map out, a terrain of suffering.

I am attempting here an essay that combines the passion of personal experience with reflection upon the cross in some parts of the Christian theological tradition. (I have relegated the personal experience out of which this book grew to the Afterword. Some readers might prefer to start there.) The goal is to arrive at a theologically grounded sense of hope in the face of suffering. This is a theology that hovers, as it were, at the intersection between speculation and spirituality, between the questioning of the mind and the yearnings of the heart. It is of personal provenance, but seeks to reach out to the suffering of others and to ask not simply what Christian doctrine has to say about it, but how Christian imagination can function to help us meet the darkness of suffering in human existence.

The Argument of this Book

This book looks toward the cross, and asks what role it can play in the imagination of Christian faith — how it might evoke both utter realism about life as it is, and a sense of hope about what God can ultimately bring out of it. My main argument is that we can only find this out by *going through* suffering, and not ducking the summons it issues to us to learn, from some of the harsh lessons that life and history force upon us, the truth about ourselves and about God.

Why this emphasis on going through suffering? First there is no real alternative when we are forced to face the brute fact of suffering. We can try to evade the pain that suffering forces upon us, and sometimes we can indeed succeed in "managing" pain or mitigating it, whether physical or psychic in nature. But even these efforts are an acknowledgment of the ultimate grip of suffering upon our lives. We must confront it and somehow deal with it. Ultimately, we must go through it. This is simply a datum, a given of human life. The question remaining, then, is how to go through it without losing a sense of hope, or, more precisely, how to find hope within the crucible of suffering.

In theological terms, I understand hope to be a theological virtue, a practice of faith the origins of which lie in God's own self-gift, and the endpoint of which is participation in divine life.[3] How, then, can people of faith arrive at a lived sense of hope within present moments of suffering, marked as these moments often are by a sense of hopelessness? The theological virtue of hope cannot simply be conjured up; it is not some heroic mustering of a "hope against hope." A hope against hope may simply be an act of desperation, or even a denial of what is the case about human life as we find it — a kind of Stoic resignation, or worse, a refusal to acknowledge what is real. Christian faith does not counsel such a form of hope. In the extreme, hoping against hope may become an expression of despair.

On the other hand, Christian faith does indeed recognize that life can be grim, and that the promises of God in Christ can seem very remote from life as we know it. The problem for Christian faith, then, becomes how to move from hope as promise to hope as a living and realized gift, and doing this without indulging in either fantasy or idealism. Differently expressed, the problem for faith is that we live within God's promise of a good end but do not yet see its full realization. This is the underlying premise of the Book of Hebrews, most dramatically made in chapter 11: "Faith is the realization of what is hoped for and evidence of things not seen" (Heb. 11:1).

There then follows a chronicle of faith, starting with Abel, running through Abraham and Sarah and their descendants, to Moses, David, and all the generations leading up to Christ: "All of these died in faith. They did not receive what had been promised but saw it and greeted it from afar and acknowledged themselves to be strangers and aliens on earth" (Heb. 11:13). The promise to which Hebrews refers, of course, is the coming of the Messiah. But even in the wake of the Christ event, we live in an interregnum, between the first appearance of the promise's fulfillment in Jesus, and its full realization at the end of time.

How can we live in hope, then, if we will surely not live to see the promises of God finally fulfilled before our very eyes? I will address this question in chapter 6, when I examine the eschatology of Ignatian imagination and how the religious imagination of St. Ignatius of Loyola works within a world that stands between divine promise and its fulfillment.

Meanwhile, we focus on the here and now, on the world of suffering. And this is where going through suffering comes into play. For, resisting any temptation to escapism, the cross of Jesus describes the hard reality of what it means to "go through." It marks the recognition of the inescapability of suffering, but also the fact that suffering is a portal into the realization of the promises of God. The cross does not ask for masochism, but does force us to face what we must face in life. It is in the facing of the real, the concrete, in going through it, that we become something other than what we once were, and that we thereby can move in hope toward the promise realized. We can therefore know the joy that comes only of *having gone through*.

This is the conviction that Christian faith professes when it points to the cross as the way to the joy promised by God, the joy that is the fruit of a life of hope. Christian faith does not call for passive submission to suffering; that would be tantamount to the sacrifice of our autonomous freedom and dignity before God. However, an active obedience to reality, one in which we drive into the heart of what faces us, embrace it, and then pass through it, is essential to discovering and living the virtue of hope. In short, we arrive at hope by going through the real. All of this is expressed in flesh and blood, in the incarnation that culminated in the suffering of Jesus on the wood of the cross.

The Path of This Book

The terminology of "the real" and of "reality" figure prominently in this book. In the first instance I mean by the real the inescapable flesh-and-blood, time-and-space-bound parameters of human existence, what Christian faith holds to be the theater of the incarnation of the Son: the world as we know it. But, as the Nicene Creed so importantly states, the real, creation, includes not only what is seen, but what is unseen. It includes the depths of reality as we experience it on an empirical plane, what the theologian Karl Rahner has called the "transcendent depths" of human existence. And so, when I speak of "going through" the real in this book, I am referring, first, to facing the reality of life's sufferings full throttle, moving into the heat of suffering's furnace; but I am also referring to moving into the depths, where that suffering can take us: the transcendent depths that lead to a joyful wisdom, even an unwanted wisdom. This, it strikes me, is partly what the cross signifies.

A Christian theological approach to suffering, then, does not simply embrace the cross, but reads suffering in light of the cross. But the cross itself must be seen as a moment within the great sweep of life described by the paschal mystery: from the divine intention in the incarnation, through the life of loving suffering of Jesus revealed on the cross, and through the death of the cross toward a resurgence of life. Our intention here is to trace a movement of hope, through suffering, that can lead to authentic joy.

This book is divided into three main parts. In Part One, "Suffering, the Great Leveler," I explore the terrain of suffering that is of concern in this book, beginning with personal encounters with suffering, and the most everyday forms of what I call the darkness of suffering, commonly encountered in loss, illness, and death. Chapter 1 starts out by discussing the terrain of dark suffering — what it includes, and what we are, in fact, focusing upon in this book. For it is abundantly clear that the terrain of suffering is vast, and that only by narrowing

our focus and controlling our navigation can we glean any benefit
from our theological investigations into this vast topic.

In chapter 2, I move to a consideration of the fact that we must
face suffering, the reality of darkness as it enters into our lives. I
focus here on two models for penetration of the real, those of William
Lynch (d. 1987) and Jerome Miller. The first offers a theologically
informed description of how one can face reality and drive through
it toward hope. Lynch also offers a model of Christian religious imagination that I intend to carry forward in the discussion. Miller offers
a philosophically informed description of driving into reality, and
reaching a position of "prostration" before the sacred. Prostration is
neither submission nor obedience. It is a reverential posture born
of a courageous and humble facing of the reality of human life as
it is. Together, these two thinkers offer a phenomenology of suffering that situates it precisely where it is most directly felt: in the
deeply personal realms where suffering hits home in the hearts of
individual human persons. Obedience to the reality of suffering, particularly that brought about by tragic reversal, can lead the sufferer
closer to the realm of the sacred. But the path toward that end is an
arduous one.

In Part II, "God and the Crosses of Suffering," I explore a theological response to the terrain of suffering, and call on the theology
of Karl Rahner (d. 1984) to explore where this understanding of suffering and of the need to face it leads the Christian imagination: to
an encounter with the cross. This begins with the search for God in
the midst of suffering, and the discovery of God as empathic love.

In chapter 3, I focus on the human search for God in the midst
of dark suffering. But this search for God takes place within the
framework of the cross itself. Here we look at the cross in Christian
imagination, relying especially on the work of the German theologian
Dorothee Sölle (d. 2003). For, as Sölle demonstrates, suffering, in its
many forms, automatically raises the question of where God stands
in relation to it. There is need for an imaginative leap, beyond philosophical explanations of suffering, into the terrain of existence itself,
where God is either found or not. I examine traditional approaches to
this problem, particularly those put forth by theodicy, a philosophic

attempt to justify the goodness of God before so much suffering, innocent and otherwise. I conclude that theodicy has its limits, and that Rahner offers a breakthrough by linking the mystery of suffering itself with the mystery of God, but in such a way that the divine empathy for those who suffer does not slip from sight.

In chapter 4, I explore the place of God in relation to human suffering. Using AIDS as a metaphor for the historical and social scope of suffering, I then show how Rahner's own theology of the cross, and what he calls "Christian pessimism," can root the Christian imagination squarely within the concrete reality of suffering, facing it without blinking. Rahner offers a counsel of the cross that does not evade reality as it is, yet also offers an opening toward hopefulness. For human existence itself is the terrain where the cross looms in Christian imagination: a place where God is frighteningly absent yet also mysteriously present.

I then turn to an application of this Rahnerian theology of the cross in the context of the experience of gay and lesbian Catholics, and the counsel of the cross that is offered them by the Roman Catholic Church. In church teaching, gay Catholics are described as people beset by suffering by virtue of their condition. The Roman Magisterium recommends the cross, or a certain understanding of it, as a way of life for the gay Catholic. After an examination of this counsel of the cross, I will ask whether a compassionate tenderness is not more conducive to a path toward joy that includes the cross. Here again, Rahner, in his theology of the cross, will offer some helpful guidelines.

The final chapter constitutes the whole of Part Three. Here I turn to the imagination of Ignatius of Loyola in the Spiritual Exercises, and in particular the meditation on the incarnation. For it is only in light of the incarnation, the claim that God became human, that the cross makes any final sense. Correlatively, the cross makes sense of the incarnation, giving the enfleshment of God its finality and purpose. The Ignatian imagination serves as a bridge between the concreteness of life here on earth, and a hope that is at once transcendent yet ever being revealed within human existence. There is at work in the Ignatian imagination a dynamic eschatology, a movement through the sufferings of earthly existence toward the fulfillment of the divine promise. I suggest that the Christian horizon can lead to hope if we broaden it beyond facing our own sufferings to facing and entering into the sufferings of the world.

In the end, relying on Jon Sobrino's Ignatian-inspired theology, I propose a spirituality of the cross that includes three major moments: the relationship of the cross to the entire paschal mystery (including the enfleshment of the divine); the cross as an utterly real symbol — a symbol of the reality of suffering that culminates in death; and the cross as symbol of hope. In the concrete, this hope is realized in living a faith where, in Sobrino's memorable image, people take one another down from their crosses of suffering. This solidarity is the historical realization of the promise of the resurrection itself. Such an eschatology offers a vision of God's future that is already being realized, for in mutual solidarity, human beings find themselves already rising, already being raised by God in the "practice" of the resurrection. The path to joy through the suffering of the cross is found by embracing those who suffer, going through it with them, and moving together toward the horizon of God.

Karl Rahner as Central Inspiration

There are several interlocutors at work in this book: William Lynch, Jerome Miller, Dorothee Sölle, and Jon Sobrino chief among them. But the central interlocutor, especially in the second part of the book, is the towering theologian of twentieth-century Catholic theology, Karl Rahner.

Although this book is not simply an exposition of Rahner's theology, it pivots on Rahner's theology and spirituality. There are several reasons for this selection.

First, Rahner's is a solidly Christ-centered theology, pushing through the central motifs of the revelation of God in Jesus, and finding their focus and meaning in the interstices of human existence. A theology such as this, rooted in the real, centered on Christ, and clarified in human existence itself, can point us beyond the present situation toward a horizon of hope and ground a compassionate response to human suffering.

Yet some commentators have suggested that Rahner's theology is insufficiently grounded in the concrete, that despite his insistence on "categorical" mediations of transcendental experience, the real contours of human existence, and especially suffering, are insufficiently treated in his writings. As Dennis Marshall has convincingly shown, however, such misconceptions fall wide of the mark.[4] Marshall also demonstrates that Rahner's theology is very much concerned with the problem of suffering, including the historical concreteness of suffering, and that this can be traced to some of his earliest writings. Marshall makes several intriguing observations. Among the most important of these is that those critics who have maintained that Rahner's transcendental method gives short shrift to the historical concreteness of suffering and feeds into a sort of idealism or even a spiritualization of suffering and human experience, have misunderstood Rahner's fundamental project. According to Marshall, Rahner's aim was to pose a challenge to and a critique of just such a "modern" intellectualist tendency in the face of suffering. In place of such idealisms, Marshall argues, Rahner is trying to bring theology back to its starting point and foundation in the experience of God as Mystery, the experience of the God of Abraham, Isaac, and Jacob, and of Jesus rather than the god of the philosophers.

Second, Rahner's attention to suffering cannot be evaluated on the basis of quantifying the titles actually devoted to the topic. "Why Does God Allow Us to Suffer?" (discussed in chapter 3) is his most obvious theological treatment of theodicy, to be sure, but suffering and the problem of evil are a silent river streaming through his work.[5] Marshall correctly argues that Rahner is concerned not so much with the *why* of suffering as he is with *how* human beings, particularly those who call themselves Christian, can live with it. Experience, not theory, has priority in Rahner's theological treatment of suffering, and that includes fundamentally the experience of God.

To take this one step further, I would argue that Rahner's is an "existential" theology, planted firmly within the contours of human existence, indeed in what he terms the categorical dimensions of life.[6] Reference to his transcendental method is a way of expressing the fact that he starts out with the human, what is common to all human beings in the spiritual constitution or makeup of their lives. While he can be criticized for failing to advert with much obvious frequency and in a direct way to historical events of suffering, such as the Holocaust, he does very much appreciate that suffering involves many dimensions of life, not just the spiritual or psychological dimensions, much less only the physical.

Third, as we shall see, Rahner is a stark realist, unblinking in the face of the tragedies and incomprehensibilities of life. It is this realism, even a certain brand of pessimism, that I wish to incorporate into a renewed Christian imagination of the cross. The phrase "Christian pessimism" flows from his own pen, and offers entrée into his religious and theological imagination. At the same time, it is this very realism that allows for an optimism that correlates not with utopianism, but with the theological virtue of hope, and helps move the sufferer from the present moment of darkness into a realization of the promise giving rise to that hope.

And fourth, Rahner's own religious imagination is imbued with the cross. This is due in no small measure to his Jesuit background, for in the apostolic mysticism of St. Ignatius of Loyola, the cross and the suffering it portends color every moment in life's pilgrimage. This is due to the fact that the cross is related to every other dimension of the life of Christ, not least to the incarnation, where suffering begins, and to the resurrection, where it is finally overcome in the full meaning of a human life realized within the love of God. The influence of the cross upon Rahner's theological imagination has therefore sometimes been underestimated, as has his theological concern for human suffering. The position taken here is in contrast to that of Hans Urs von Balthasar, for example, who maintains that Rahner's transcendental Christology seems to favor the drama of the incarnation, but does not adequately admit the negative decisiveness of the cross. The cross, von Balthasar argues, is simply included within an incarnational design that "determines in advance the place of the cross in this system...."[7] As I hope these pages will demonstrate, I find this type of view to reflect a fundamental misunderstanding of the nature of Rahner's overall theological project and the role that the cross plays within it.

How, then, can Rahner's theological project function here? First, we are undertaking a theological reflection that takes seriously the concreteness of the human experience of suffering as a place where the holiness of God can be encountered. My point of departure, therefore, is existential, or within the realm of what Rahner termed the *existentiell*.[8] While I count myself among those theologians still partial to Rahner's transcendental subjectivity as a valid point of departure for theological reflection, I wish to focus the starting point upon what he called the categorical — concrete, historical mediations of this transcendental experience — or what I am naming here the reality of suffering. In conversation with other theological voices, Rahner can contribute to the construction of a theology of the cross that addresses the reality of suffering and, at the same time, offers grounds for hope.

◆ ◆ ◆

While it is my intention that this book might be of some help to others who are facing their own sufferings, or who are trying to face the sufferings of the world, I readily acknowledge the highly personal origin and limited horizon of these reflections. The base from which I write might be too narrow for some people, or not congruent enough with their own experiences of life or interpretations of larger historical realities. Such is the nature of the subject matter I am trying to handle. At the same time, I want to emphasize that no matter how personal and unique our experiences of suffering may be, they visit us within larger social and historical frameworks, within the contexts of a whole suffering humanity. That is what makes our sufferings part of a manifold of suffering, one that involves us totally, but does not reduce the mystery of suffering to our own sufferings alone. Even in our private sufferings, we participate in the history of the groanings and hopes of the whole human race. Perhaps true tragedy occurs for Christians when they lose sight of the conviction that their sufferings can be an invitation to solidarity with all those who suffer, all the victims of any darkness, and that God can be encountered there. For the Christian is reminded that "neither death, nor life, nor angels, nor principalities, nor present things, nor future things, nor powers, nor height, nor depth, nor any other creature will be able to separate us from the love of God in Christ Jesus our Lord" (Rom. 8:38–39). But the path to gaining that insight is an arduous one, and the wisdom contained in that statement is not one we eagerly seek, for it requires that we face our sufferings and go through them, with others, in a spirit of hope that we may never see fully realized.

Acknowledgments

This book has been a long brewing project, and my thanks to many people extends quite far back in time. It is probably best simply to list the people and institutions who have made it possible for me to complete this book:

- The Sisters of Mercy of the Americas, Auburn Regional Community, for the love shown toward my family and for inviting me to offer the Holy Week Triduum in 1993 which initiated this project.

- Santa Clara University, for granting me sabbatical time in 1996– 97 and 2004. Special thanks go to my chair, Catherine Bell, and Provost, Denise Carmody.

- The Jesuit Institute, Boston College, for a fellowship where I pursued the theological implications of AIDS, and explored Rahner's Christian pessimism, some of the results of which appear here, especially in chapter 4.

- Dr. Roman Siebenrock, Karl Rahner Archiv, University of Innsbruck, for assistance with the papers of Karl Rahner on Christian pessimism.

- Paul Locatelli, SJ, President of Santa Clara University, and the Franzia Foundation, for funding of my research into the works of William Lynch.

- Patrice Kane, archivist at Fordham University Library, for assistance with the papers of William Lynch.

- The Karl Rahner Society, for the invitation to deliver a paper on Rahner's Christian pessimism at the Catholic Theological Society of America meeting, June 1995.

- The faculty and students at Weston Jesuit School of Theology, Cambridge, Massachusetts, where I was able to present some of these thoughts in seminars and faculty forums between 2001 and 2003.

- Dr. Bob Voglewede, Director of Mission Services, Avera Health Care, Sioux Falls, South Dakota, for the invitation to deliver some of these thoughts at the 20th Annual Avera Health Ethics Conference, April 1, 2004.

- Stephen A. Privett, SJ, President of the University of San Francisco, for offering the hospitality of the university and its libraries during the Fall Semester, 2004.

- Denise Carmody and Tom Powers, SJ, for critically reading drafts of this book and offering their suggestions for improvement; and Tom Beaudoin, Douglas Burton-Christie, Sidney Callahan, James Keenan, SJ, and Richard Rodriguez.

- Frank Oveis, Continuum International Publishing Group, for ongoing and constant encouragement.

- Joel Dorius, Michael J. Buckley, SJ, and John Murphy, SJ, for invaluable conversations about these topics over several years.

- The Jesuit Community at Santa Clara University, for so much support.

Last, but not least, I thank my mother, Doris Crowley, who has more than earned her own "unwanted wisdom," and whose courage, hope, and joy in life have provided me unforgettable inspiration.

Santa Clara University
Santa Clara, California
May 1, 2005

Part One

Suffering,
the Great Leveler

Chapter One

The Terrain of Suffering

All thought must be interrupted by the great counterexperiences of suffering. To develop a logos on theos — a theology — today is to start by facing evil and suffering.[1]
— David Tracy

SUFFERING IS the great leveler, cutting across all stations and divisions of human life and, in a real sense, uniting people across time. The sufferings of the present age are but the latest manifestations of the perennial lot of the human race. Nevertheless, suffering now presents itself as a problem for theology and for religious belief, as well as for philosophical speculation, on a scale that has perhaps not been seen since the appearance of the great theodicies in the sixteenth century. The sacred scriptures of many religious traditions, major speculative thinkers, and great artists, writers, and photographers have addressed the reality of suffering as a part of the human experience. But it is the modern era, at least that part of it extending from the Enlightenment onward, and especially the manifestations of suffering that came on the heels of the industrial and technological revolutions, new forms of warfare, and the advent of modern political and economic systems — notably fascist and totalitarian regimes of repression — that have posed questions to the religions, and to Christian faith in particular, that no theology can ignore. When Johannes Metz famously asked how one might speak of God after Auschwitz,[2] he was speaking from a new theological place, one where the starting point is the conundrum of suffering and the mystery of evil of which it is an expression. Not always even an issue for theology, suffering would now become the starting point for mounting a credible Christian theological viewpoint. Suffering, understood in Roger Haight's phrase, as the "negativity of human existence" seen in the victims of racism, sexism, and social injustice, would motivate the theologies of black and mestizo theologians in this country, Latin American and other liberation theologians, feminist (and womanist and mujerista) theologians, and gay theologians, among others. As Haight observes:

> Although human suffering cannot be reduced to social suffering, liberation christologies, including feminist, black, and womanist christologies, have brought to the fore at its most telling point the problem of evil and suffering for christology. The negativity of human existence reaches its most mysterious, widespread, and scandalous form in social suffering and oppression imposed by human beings on other innocent human beings.[3]

In a similar vein, Edward Schillebeeckx speaks of " . . . the negative depth of what finitude and finite freedom can involve."[4]

The dawn of AIDS would bring together a whole nexus of sufferings — physical, social, psychological, economic, and existential — of the sort that could only come together in a plague.[5] This particular plague, or, more properly speaking, epidemic, was made more complex by virtue of its sexual transmission, especially in its early phases among gay men, so that sexuality itself became seen as a locus of human suffering, some of which gave rise to the disease itself. This entire theater of suffering — from wars and genocides to plagues and pandemics — has called for a theological response to the reality of suffering, on both its personal and historical scales, that no one could have anticipated at the dawn of the twentieth century. And now we are in a new century, one that is already scarred by new forms of suffering, not least the ubiquity of fear present in the form of terrorism's constant threat and the unleashing of new wars around the world. There is truth in the saying that there is "nothing new under the sun" (Eccles. 1:9) in any of this. But what is new, at least for Christian theology, is that suffering has become a point of departure, a factum before which not only God, but faith itself, must be justified. Theology can no longer remain silent in the face of the massive suffering that has descended upon the human race.

The Scope of Our Attention

What do we mean by suffering? This is not the place to review the mountain of writing that has already been given over to the topic, nor merely to repeat what has already been said. But I would like to stress two points here. The first is that suffering is not simply a problem to be solved. It cannot be solved; it is wrapped up within the mystery of evil itself, and therefore presents itself as a "mystery," a reality that can be unfolded almost limitlessly but never finally exhausted, much less fully controlled. Our efforts at theologizing about it inevitably confront the limits of the finite mind before a perpetual enigma.

The second point is that suffering is irreducibly personal, and although suffering certainly manifests social and historical dimensions, it cannot be understood on the social and historical planes alone, as if it could be captured objectively; it always involves the suffering of human beings in ineluctably personal and unique ways. This is not to say that it can be limited to an individual's world of experience; it is to say that we cannot afford to ignore the ultimately personal dimension of human suffering. Such a view was suggested by Schillebeeckx: "One can objectify a problem and take one's distance from it; this makes a detached explanation possible. But suffering and evil in our human history are also *my* suffering, *my* evil, *my* agony and *my* death. They cannot be objectified."[6]

The point again is that we are dealing with mystery when we are dealing with suffering, something that eludes a final mapping or explanation. While we are always mindful of the broad historical stage of human suffering in the forms of war, plague, genocide, and natural disasters like earthquakes and tsunamis, we are also mindful that even historical forms of suffering arrive upon human beings in the uniqueness of their lives. It is actual human beings who suffer, not simply groups or classes of people, or populations. This is what makes suffering "dark" for all of those who suffer, even those who suffer in the company of others. As long as it remains "my" suffering, then there is a sense in which I cannot escape the fact that I myself am suffering. I am enveloped by a world of suffering from which there can at times seem to be no exit. But it is only when we recognize this aspect of suffering that we can enter into a compassionate response to suffering, to people who, like me, suffer. As Jon Sobrino has put it, "We cannot be human without making suffering and compassion central to our life."[7]

But what does it mean to suffer? Or, perhaps better: what does "suffering" mean?

The word "suffer" (and its derivative, "suffering,") tell us something about the matter of which we speak. The word comes from two Latin roots: *sub*, meaning "under" or "beneath" and *ferre* meaning "to bear." So the general sense of the word is to bear something, to undergo, or to endure. The *Oxford English Dictionary* defines the verb "to suffer" as "to have (something painful, distressing, or injurious) inflicted or imposed upon one; to submit to with pain, distress, or grief" and "to go or pass through, be subject to, undergo, experience (now usually something evil or painful)" and "to undergo or submit to pain, punishment, or death."[8] The main idea here is not simply that suffering entails that which we find "unpleasant," but that what is unpleasant comes upon us against our wills. We are forced, as it were, to undergo, or to endure, that which we would rather not have to face.

So, what is it that we endure against our wills? How do we suffer? Keeping in mind that no one approach can contain the whole of it, I would nevertheless suggest several ways people can be said to suffer. The most fundamental form of suffering is the experience of loss and the consequent grief that flows from it. Indeed, loss in some sense establishes the template for most other forms of suffering. Beyond loss itself, we will discuss various other dimensions of suffering, such as those revealed in disease, illness, and physical pain, psychic, pain and affliction, and pain shared on broad social and historic scales. All of these forms of suffering entail not only loss, but also the threat of utter hopelessness. They all contribute to the darkness of suffering.

28

The darkness of suffering includes as well various natural, psychic, and historical forms of suffering. Natural suffering may be caused by objective forces completely beyond our control, such as natural calamities, or by mixed factors, some involving human agency, such as diseases and injuries. Its most immediate and obvious manifestation is pain, not only bodily, but also psychic. Closely associated with this level of suffering, then, is what might be called "spiritual" suffering, where the person experiences disorder and disharmony, even moral upheaval, in the wake of the waves of pain. For example, anguish and anxiety may well attend the onset and progress of serious disease. The suffering that attends the death of persons close to us can trigger such a degree of spiritual suffering that God no longer seems to register as a reality in one's life; God seems remote, if not entirely absent. A third dimension could be called historical or social suffering, where personal and structural elements of life conspire to bring about a diminishment of human dignity. These would include systems of economic or social injustice, political or religious oppression, or denial of either who one is, or even that one exists. In many people's lives, these dimensions of suffering converge, so that natural, spiritual, and historical dimensions work together to grind down the human person, reducing her to a suffering pulp, or even whole peoples to dust. We need only look at the results of famine and genocide in East Africa, compounded as it has been by both war and disease, to see evidence of this kind of suffering — not an abstraction, but endured by actual human persons, both together and in their irreducible uniqueness. In all of these forms of suffering taking place on the historical stage, individual persons suffer at the core of their souls. They find themselves lost amidst a wilderness of pain shared by others. Yet, for each of them, the pain of the world is inescapably my pain.

What I am concerned about here is the suffering that people endure at the core of their souls by virtue of living through and enduring any form of dark suffering. I would like to keep the focus of this work on the individual person, the one who suffers, precisely within the reality of their historical situations. However, I do not think we necessarily have to turn to the most extreme forms of suffering to suggest that suffering can, in the aggregate, reduce people to shadows of themselves. Even in its more "ordinary" forms, such as grief and chronic illness, suffering can tend toward and even succeed in reducing a person to nothing. An unremitting degenerative disease, or a string of losses, can finally take a toll so great as to leave a person gutted, even despairing, utterly bereft of any sense of hope, and even of faith itself. It is this quality of suffering, its capacity for an absolute diminishment, of ultimate loss, that I wish to take as a point of departure. For, in whatever form it is encountered, this is what constitutes the essence of suffering.

Loss

There is a great deal of literature on the suffering generated by loss, especially loss to death, and the grief that follows such loss. This is not the place to rehearse all of that collected wisdom, which in any case would be an impossible task. Furthermore, insight into the suffering of loss and grief is not an arcane wisdom. Anyone who has ever lost a loved one to death knows something of this kind of suffering. When we meet the intransigence of death, we also face the altered state of life which it forces upon us. Karl Rahner wrote movingly of the unfolding experience of the loss of loved ones over the course of his own life:

> ... [T]he true process of my life consists only of those bound together by real love, and this column grows ever shorter and more quiet, until one day I myself will have to break off from the line of march and leave without a word or wave of farewell, never more to return.
>
> That's why my heart is now with them, with my loved ones who have taken their leave of me. There is no substitute for them; there are no others who can fill the vacancy when one of those whom I have really loved, suddenly and unexpectedly departs and is with me no more. In true love no one replaces another, for true love loves the other person in that depth where he is uniquely and irreplaceably himself. And thus, as death has

trodden roughly through my life, every one of the departed has taken a piece of my heart with him and often enough my whole heart.[9]

There is indeed a real sadness, emptiness, and pain which we have a right to admit when we encounter the unanswerableness of death, perhaps more so when it comes on the heels of a tragic reversal in the lives of those who have died. There is no virtue, and certainly nothing particularly Christian, in denying for a moment the harsh sense of finality death imposes on each of us.

Centuries earlier, St. Bernard of Clairvaux would interrupt his discourse on the Song of Songs because grief over the loss of his brother, a fellow monk, was piercing his heart to the degree that he could not continue his academic discourse on the Bible's great ode to love:

How long shall I keep my pretence [sic] while a hidden fire burns my sad heart, consumes me from within? A concealed fire creeps forward with full play, it rages more fiercely. I, whose life is bitterness, what have I to do with this canticle? Overpowering sorrow distracts my mind, the displeasure of the Lord drains my spirit dry. For when he was taken away, he who enabled me to attend to the study of spiritual doctrine so freely and so frequently, my heart departed from me too. But up till now I have done violence to myself and kept up a pretence, lest my affection should seem stronger than my faith. . . . You, my sons, know how deep my sorrow is, how galling the wound it leaves. . . . My brother by blood, but bound to me more intimately by religious profession. Share my mourning with me, you who know these things.[10]

And, in more recent times, perhaps the most poignant example of the literature on loss and grief is C. S. Lewis's *A Grief Observed,* which he wrote after the death of his wife, Joy. Lewis feels his loss not only in his heart, but in his body and in his soul: "No one ever told me that grief felt so like fear. I am not afraid, but the sensation is like being afraid. The same fluttering in the stomach, the same restlessness, the yawning. I keep on swallowing."[11]

What manner of suffering is this? It is the suffering of someone who has lost a tremendous good, the good of another person's life. And that good is not only the good of the deceased; their good is also *my* good, what helps make my life a good thing. I know the good that has been lost because I possess that good myself. The loss of such a great good through death comes as the incursion of a most unwelcome reality into our lives. By virtue of the fact that it robs us of a good, it comes as an expression of evil, a privation of the good. In the loss of someone to death, we are invaded by an enemy that, however naturally it may come, as in the form of cancer, nevertheless robs people of a very great good, life itself. This is why the suffering of loss can also be felt outside of death itself, in so many other forms where evil as privation of the good robs us of our ownmost good, as for example, in the loss of health, or of a house, or the loss that comes from a personal violation like rape. All of these are marked by the involuntary loss of an intrinsic good through the incursion of an evil into our lives. This experience of loss of an intrinsic good to some uninvited form of evil, coming as an alien invader to steal away this good, and with it, a part of ourselves, is the most basic kind of suffering, and lies at the heart of all other forms of suffering, including the suffering that visits humanity on the widest historical planes. Suffering is first and foremost the experience of the involuntary loss of an intrinsic good.

Illness and Physical Pain

Illness, involuntary loss of that form of the good we call health, is a pervasive form of suffering for all human beings, for some clearly more than others. This is a very difficult terrain to chart, because illness, the name for the suffering that attends any disease of the body, is multi-layered and extremely complex, involving many dimensions of the human person — not only the corporeal, but the psychic, social, and spiritual dimensions as well. To separate these dimensions of illness from one another is to engage in an artificial partitioning, for in reality these conspire to constitute illness. Nevertheless, I will first focus on the corporeal dimension before passing on to those dimensions of illness, because it is necessary to take each of these into account, on their own terms, as it were, if only for purposes of gaining a preliminary understanding.

The first thing we naturally note about physical illness is that it affects the body: the physical body suffers. The body has been likened to a machine, the most awesome machine ever contrived, and, like a machine, something that can be fixed, analogous to the way a mechanic repairs a car. But, as we know, it is so much more than that, as anyone who has been ill or tended someone who is seriously ill knows very well. What, then, is the nature of bodily suffering? What is it that makes of physical illness a form of suffering itself? Why do we not just accept illness as a natural phenomenon, something that comes with life as it is, and leave it at that?

This brings us back to the essence of suffering. For we are speaking here not only of something that occurs within nature, but of an experience: the experience of the involuntary loss of a good, in this case, the good of health itself.[12] A person who suffers multiple handicaps knows very well what such a loss entails, because the body simply will not work the way it was intended to. When St. Francis of Assisi referred to his body as "Brother Ass" he was in a sense standing outside himself and looking at a body that was the source of a great deal of frustration: his body would not cooperate with the desires of his soul, and he suffered terribly as a result. In a certain sense, his bodily illnesses diminished him as a person, because his person depended so much on the body in order to show itself and to function within space and time. The body in illness is therefore a constant source of frustration and involuntary diminishment.

But illness involves more than frustration and diminishment; it often also involves pain. Pain in some form is the key symptom of virtually all illness, and is also the strongest marker of suffering. And, as we know, even the most mundane pain, such as the pain of a toothache, is in its own way unbearable, in-sufferable, because it is all we can think about while it is happening: it almost completely robs us of our peace, our sense of the good of health we once knew.[13] All we can think of is getting rid of it — yearning for a state of painlessness, like the one we knew before the onset of this or that particular pain. And we will do almost anything we can to relieve ourselves of the pain, to restore some semblance of health, which we rightly associate with painlessness. The alleviation of suffering ordinarily entails the alleviation of pain that may either attend suffering, or in fact be the cause of it.

But the main point here is that suffering is imposed upon persons, and persons are somatic, embodied, beings. There is no suffering, even the suffering of mental illness, that does not have its physiological correlates that are manifested often enough in a diagnosable bodily illness, or at least in a discomfort that itself constitutes a form of pain, however undefined it may be.

This pain is intimately related to the mystery of health itself, which often enough only comes to light in the throes of bodily illness and its attendant pain. In her illuminating essay, "Illness as Metaphor," the late essayist Susan Sontag (d. 2004) describes the mythology surrounding cancer which has associated it with "a steady repression of feeling," thwarted passions such as rage, and, following Wilhelm Reich, " 'a disease following emotional resignation and bioenergetic shrinking, a giving up of hope.' "[14] In her later essay, "AIDS and Its Metaphors," she explains what she was trying to achieve in the earlier essay, based on her own experience as a cancer patient: " ... [I]t was my doleful observation, repeated again and again, that the metaphoric trappings that deform the experience of having cancer have very real consequences: they inhibit people from seeking treatment early enough, or from making a greater effort to get competent treatment. The metaphors and myths, I was convinced, kill."[15] And William Lynch, writing out of his own nervous breakdown, speaks of the dangers of digging "too deep the psychological walls and moats between the well and the ill."[16] "For it is a fact, and it is the greatest hope of the sick, that there is nothing wrong with them that is not human and is not present in some degree in every member of the race."[17]

The German philosopher Hans Georg Gadamer (d. 2002) holds, rather, that we must come to see health itself as an enigma, a state of "hidden harmony" that becomes thematic precisely in the face of illness. For this reason we must be on guard against objectifying illness, as opposed to health, for illness itself is a state that presents itself only in relation to the elusive ideal of health:

> Even when we say that we have succeeded in "mastering" or controlling an illness, it is as if we are separating the illness off from the person involved. The illness is treated as if it possesses an independent existence which we must seek to destroy. This takes on a specific meaning when we think on a larger scale, as for example about great epidemics. . . . [W]e must recognize that health always stands within a broader horizon of permanent jeopardy and potential disturbance.[18]

It is this murky zone between illness and health that is itself a source of suffering, especially encountered when people struggle to regain the elusive equilibrium of health.

Psychic Pain

In our discussion of the suffering of illness and pain in the previous section, we moved quite naturally into the next region of dark suffering, that of psychic pain. For strongly associated with the physical suffering we call illness and its attendant pain is the suffering that takes place in the interior parts of a person who is ill. Where some sense of order and orientation once governed, there may now reign a sense of disorder, of de-centering, and growing fear and anxiety over the eventual outcome of the ordeal of the pain of illness. A sense of darkness, despondency, and even of despair can set in, a sense of entrapment, or of what Sartre called "No-Exit." In the extreme, it is at this juncture that death can seem preferable to the suffering one feels forced to endure and from which there is seemingly no escape.

The religious and political essayist Simone Weil (d. 1943) had a word for this kind of suffering. She called it "affliction" (*le mal-heur*). In her essay "The Love of God and Affliction," Weil maintains that affliction is "inseparable from physical suffering" or pain, but involves psychic and social elements as well.[19] The physical part of affliction corresponds to the pain found in suffering in general. By "pain" Weil means in the first instance physical suffering, something endured that results in a diminution of the physical and psychic integrity of the person. Weil herself suffered for years from intensive migraine headaches, and although these in themselves did not constitute what she terms "affliction," as physical pain they were certainly representative of an ingredient in what she means by the term. Weil describes her headaches as both a physical event and entrée into heightened spiritual awareness:

> In 1938 I spent ten days at Solesmes, from Palm Sunday to Easter Tuesday, following all the liturgical services. I was suffering from splitting headaches; each sound hurt me like a blow; by an extreme effort of concentration I was able to rise above this wretched flesh, to leave it to suffer by itself, heaped up in a corner, and to find a pure and perfect joy in the unimaginable beauty of the chanting and the words. This experience enabled me by analogy to get a better understanding of the possibility of loving divine love in the midst of affliction. It goes without saying that in the course of these services the thought of the Passion of Christ entered into my being once and for all.[20]

While she is referring to physical pain here, elsewhere — sounding a bit like C. S. Lewis in his description of grief — she is clear that "pain" can also be understood analogously to physical pain:

> Even in the case of the absence or death of someone we love, the irreducible part of the sorrow is akin to physical pain, a difficulty in breathing, a constriction of the heart, an unsatisfied need, hunger, or the almost biological disorder caused by the brutal liberation of some energy, hitherto directed by an attachment and now left without a guide. A sorrow that is not centered around an irreducible core of such a nature is mere romanticism or literature.[21]

Psychic pain, so closely lined to physical pain, is a real thing, not imaginary. As a reality and as an element of affliction, it is unremitting in its claims upon the human person. It finally succeeds in reducing the afflicted person in humiliation to the form of its slave, so that the one who suffers is permanently "branded" by it.[22] This humiliation itself is a form of pain, " . . . a violent condition of the whole corporal being, which longs to surge up under the outrage but is forced, by impotence or fear, to hold itself in check."[23] Those who suffer chronic, progressively debilitating, or crippling diseases can easily succumb to the feeling that they are in fact being subjected to a humiliation that cannot be countered. Perhaps not entirely unlike the torture victim, a scream surges from within, desperate to find its voice, but remains muffled, silent to the outside world. If the degeneration is progressive and unrelenting, it threatens to take away everything, pointing the sufferer mercilessly towards her own death.

But, Weil says, we have "only" pain and not affliction "unless the event that has seized and uprooted a life attacks it, directly or indirectly, in all its parts, social, psychological and physical."[24] Thus, the same event, such as suffering from cancer, might lead one person into the depths of affliction, but leave another "only" within the realm of pain.[25] Affliction, however, entails an "uprooting of life" and the forcing of the person, against her will, to her own Golgatha of complete abandonment, life on the edge of despair, or perhaps lodged deeply within it. Even Jesus was forced "to implore that he might be spared, to seek consolation from man, to believe he was forsaken by the Father."[26] The suffering of affliction is of necessity, therefore, also a spiritual suffering, for to be led to the cross can imply that God allows "the souls of the innocent to be seized by the force of evil. . . . "[27] This leaves the afflicted one grasping for words and feeling situated beyond the reach of compassion. "Except for those whose whole soul is inhabited by Christ," the afflicted are mutilated, spurned and despised.[28] The soul becomes affliction's "accomplice," and God seems utterly absent, leaving the sufferer nothing to love.[29] And the afflicted are in turn despised by those who are spared it, those whom we call "well." This in turn can lead to self-hatred, guilt, and a sense of defilement at the core of the soul. One's ownmost nature may be "irremediably wounded."[30]

Here we are at the heart of the agony of suffering: Where the one who suffers feels avoided or even rejected because she is no longer among the normal and healthy.[31] And the internalization of the pain is so totalizing as to seem inescapable.

Shared Social Suffering

Gadamer's reference to the great epidemics is a reminder that even illness is rarely only a matter of one's own isolated suffering. Thus far I have been referring to suffering as loss of the good, of *my* good, particularly in the forms of illness, pain, and attendant psychic distress. But in very, very few instances in human life is suffering only "my" problem: it is also "our" problem. It is the loss not only of "my" good, but also of "our" good. This is one of the insights people gain when tending to and accompanying someone who is dying, all the way through the process. We are acutely aware that this is the irreducibly unique and privileged moment in that person's life; at the same time it is a shared moment, a shared time. Very little that happens to any of us is so private, so much my own problem, that it does not have ripple effects. And sometimes our sufferings are shared in such a way that we realize that we are participating in much larger forms of suffering. We see this, for example, when we look at plagues or epidemics (like malaria, AIDS, or even some forms of cancer) where suffering can no longer be treated only as a personal matter alone. We also see it in the fate of undocumented persons struggling to survive, in the suffering of abused children, boy soldiers and girl sex workers, and those who suffer the real effects of discrimination such as racism, sexism, and homophobia. As David Tracy has observed: "The attention of many has been turned away from modern self-confidence to face the evils and sufferings of whole peoples — the colonization of the Americas, Africa, and parts of Asia and Oceania; the horrors of the Middle Passage; the famines of Ireland and Russia; the Armenian massacres; the Gulag Archipelago; Cambodia; the AIDS plague; Bosnia. On and on the list runs with relentless severity."[32]

Suffering is shared, suffering is social, suffering is historical in its scope. This raises the issue, of course, that suffering is the result not only of what we endure, what comes upon us through the forces of nature, but also of what we do to others and what others do to us. That is, there is quite often a moral or ethical dimension to suffering that we tend to overlook in wanting to treat it as a pathology, or, in the case of illness, as a medical problem alone. Some forms of suffering, such as those already mentioned, but also those obvious historic forms of suffering such as war, torture, terrorism, or genocide, have a clear moral etiology.[33] They derive from the human soul, and implicate the body and psyche, and whole peoples, in the involuntary loss of good, resulting in massive suffering.

In *Horrendous Evils and the Goodness of God,* Marilyn McCord Adams gives us some examples of the social and historical scale of suffering, what she calls "horrendous evils" such as "psycho-physical torture whose ultimate goal is the disintegration of personality, betrayal of one's deepest loyalties, child abuse of the sort described by [Dostoevsky's] Ivan Karamazov, child pornography, parental incest, slow death by starvation, the explosion of nuclear bombs over populated areas."[34] Adams suggests that such forms of suffering lead us reasonably to question whether those who participate in such evils, either as suffering victims or as perpetrators, any longer have lives worth living because "it is so difficult humanly to conceive how such evils could be overcome." She continues:

> In most (if not all cases) their destructive power reaches beyond their concrete disvalue (such as the pain and material deprivation they involve), into the deep structure of the person's frameworks of meaning-making, seemingly to defeat the individual's value as a person, to degrade him/her to sub-human status. The Nazi death camps aimed, not merely to kill, but to dehumanize their victims, treating them worse than cattle to break down their personalities and reduce their social instincts to raw animal aggression and self-preservation. Organizing and running such institutions also degraded the Nazis, who caricatured human nature by using their finest powers the more imaginatively to transgress the bounds of human decency.[35]

Elaine Scarry's *The Body in Pain* similarly suggests that what most powerfully represents the horrors of war are the sufferings of its innocent victims, notably those who have been subjected to torture, the aim of which is the obliteration, or "unmaking," of the person-hood of its victims. She sums up part of her argument with a literary allusion:

> Whatever its political naiveté or its melodramatic intentions, Poe's "The Pit and the Pendulum" discovers in its final moments the single distilled form of torture that in many ways represents all forms of torture, the walls collapsing in on the human center to crush it alive.[36]

Both Adams and Scarry manage to focus upon the suffering of in-dividual persons, notably the victims, without abstracting them or their sufferings from the objective, historical (indeed horrendous) contexts in which that suffering is brought about, through human agency. There is a "historical consciousness" of suffering at work here that is indispensable to the discussion of suffering in our time. But there is also the recognition that suffering is not an abstraction, that it constitutes an inescapable reality for all people, and also threatens each of us and all of us.

This shared dimension of suffering, even though it is irreducibly personal, also points toward the exigency of solidarity, not only among those who suffer, but between the suffering and those who are, for various reasons, spared certain forms of it, at least for a time. This note of solidarity, of suffering with, is key to a Christian under-standing of suffering as a place where God can be found. We shall make note of this later in the book when we ask how or where God can be found in the midst of suffering, and what this must lead us to do about it.

Spiritual Suffering: The Threat of Hopelessness

What does this add up to for us? That, at the bottom of all these levels of suffering which we human beings face, there is the most fundamental form, and perhaps the most dreadful: a suffering of the soul. For when we are confronted with suffering in all its forms, we are also faced with the choice of either dealing with it and its con-sequences, or of finding ways to anesthetize ourselves to its pain. Of course, we want to relieve ourselves of suffering; no question. To wallow in it would indeed constitute a form of pathology. But, at the same time, we must also face the dreadful fact that the relief of symptoms, or the removal of causes, or the passage of time and the passing of some forms of suffering — do not automatically heal the deepest wounds. This is why bromides like "time heals," or "life must go on," can come off as insensitive and even cruel. The mother who has lost a child to a senseless stabbing suffers at the core of her soul for years to come; she ever feels the loss. The survivors of a village wiped out by a volcano in El Salvador will never forget. The people of Rwanda, where some 800,000 people were massacred in less than a month, will never fully recover, even as "life must go on." In all of these cases, and countless others like them, we are dealing with a fundamental crisis of hope — the almost total loss of it.

The worst form of spiritual suffering, and certainly the core of it, theologically speaking, is loss — loss of hope. According to William Lynch, a sense of hopelessness derives from the feeling that our suffering lies beyond help; we cannot even imagine or envision an alternative scenario. The result is an inability to face what is real because of a prior sense of impossibility, a sense that there are no resources, outer or inner, to call upon.[37] One feels overwhelmed and every effort to deal with it seems futile. "The striving self cannot reach the ideal self: hope is destroyed."[38] One result might be anger, and a resultant depression as that anger is either repressed unconsciously or suppressed through habits of accommodation. In the grip of depression, even if one can see what are objective sources of help, one may feel utterly helpless, and ultimately sink into a feeling of nothingness — an *apatheia* leading to inertia.

Lynch certainly does not wish to suggest that such situations of hopelessness are illusory. To the contrary, hopelessness itself is a reality. "Many things, I repeat, *are* hopeless."[39] And, as the examples of suffering cited by Marilyn McCord Adams suggest, there are some forms of evil that cause so much destruction that it is impossible to imagine a hopeful way out. And there are some people in this world who seem to be, perhaps really are, "beyond help." There seems no exit for them from their sufferings.

All the more reason, then, why a certain "Christian" ideal of perfection not be imposed as a command upon anyone. A "buck up" attitude or the Stoic "stiff upper lip" can result in non-biblical and Gnostic notions of perfection and a consequent sense of hopelessness of its ever being attained. "In fact this dilemma — I must but I cannot — is the common mark of many forms of the hopeless."[40] And this form of hopelessness cannot, of its very nature, be overcome by more striving. Just as the sufferer himself must approach reality head on through an exercise of imagination in and through appropriating help where it is to be found, so the one who would help the sufferer must approach the facts of human life in the concrete and from the inside. That is, they must understand that hopelessness is a reality, not simply a phase that one can snap out of. It is as much a reality for the person who suffers as is the "outside world" occupied by the self-proclaimed healthy.

As I earlier suggested, what makes this world of hopelessness utterly dark is the sense of imprisonment that characterizes it. Imprisonment within suffering, or feeling entrapped by it, lies at the heart of all forms of the darkest human suffering. It is what makes suffering not merely an annoyance that one can remedy on one's own. Imprisonment is linked with a sense of endlessness, like a life sentence without parole. There will be struggles between hope and forces working against hope, resulting in rage and fury which, when suppressed, become depression.[41] This is certainly true of the suffering attending illness, especially a chronic illness. Some rare and fortunate people are spared such suffering. But for the vast majority, illness ultimately befalls them, often in severe forms. And, as long as it is there, it cannot be papered over or escaped through spiritual fantasy. One in fact quite naturally may feel imprisoned within it. And when that sense of imprisonment or of entrapment leads to a diminishment of hope to the point of hopelessness, then it can descend to despair, for there is no sense of possibly escaping what has definitively descended. Sure as aging, sure as death, so sure is the iron grip of some diseases, or the irretrievable sense of loss and even of meaninglessness that sometimes ensues from them.

Here is where Simone Weil's description of the effect of affliction becomes operative: where the human being is reduced to a mere thing by virtue of what descends upon her like the force of gravity. And what one discovers at this point is the need to recover a sense of oneself, even a shred of oneself, precisely as human.[42] But how? For the true sufferer is indeed helpless, in need of help, perhaps even to imagine an "outside world" in which to place all of her suffering. And the real outside world often enough does not offer the help that is needed, and says that one's help must come from within, rationalizing: "God helps those who help themselves."[43] Yet, somehow, one must be helped to the awareness that "I am a human being, flesh and blood, even more real than the disease that afflicts me." For we are all in the dark, we are all suffering, we are all subject to the threat of hopelessness, and we are all in need of help. We all need to exercise our imaginations in order to "see" an outside world. More to the point: we all need to discover the fundamental image of hope, which is the whole human being herself, himself. How to get there will feature heavily in the pages that follow, for this ultimately relates to a Christian understanding of the future, an eschatology, firmly planted in the reality of the present.

Chapter Two

Facing the Reality of Suffering

*The richest truths are the ones
it is most excruciating for us to uncover.*[1]
— Jerome A. Miller

IN THE MEDIEVAL TOWN of Colmar, situated in the French region of Alsace, stands an old monastery that has since been converted into an art museum. The Unterlinden Museum houses a famous sixteenth-century rendering of the crucifixion by Matthias Grünewald, possibly one of the most grotesque renderings of the suffering of Jesus ever executed. One is immediately struck by the exaggeration of all the features of the agony. A crown of thorns that seems more like a small bush encircles the head of Jesus. Massive nails drive through huge gnarled hands and twisted feet. An emaciated, concave corpus, hangs from a curved beam of wood. And one can see the marks not only of the scourging and bruising Jesus endured on the way to the cross, but also something very peculiar: bluish skin lesions scattered all over his body. Such lesions were not uncommon among the peasants of that region in the sixteenth century, the result of a rye fungus, ergot, that was carried in the grains grown in that region. In addition to the skin lesions, sufferers displayed "inflated bellies and gangrenous limbs...."[2]

Grünewald had painted this particular crucifixion as part of a poly-tych for a hospital chapel run by a religious order in nearby Isenheim, where those in the region suffering from ergot were taken for pallia-tive care. Presumably they were brought to the hospital chapel where, during Mass, they could gaze on this rendering of the suffering Christ who was himself afflicted with their own awful disease. The altarpiece rather forced them to gaze head on into the inescapable reality of their disease, but also to see it as something borne by Jesus himself. It was thus understood as a pervasive disease the horrors of which reached even Christ. Those horrors, vividly obvious in the painful lesions, are joined to the horror of the cross itself. Jesus on the cross thereby assumes the marks of the disease, and suffers it, thereby joining in solidarity with the agony of all its victims. There was seemingly no escaping it, but only facing it through the religious imagination — and thereby Christ's own sufferings of the very same malady, and his identification with those who suffered from it in the region of Colmar, could lead to some sense of consolation and perhaps even hope.

On another panel of this polytych the same artist painted two other scenes: a most unusual nativity scene, where the Christ child is serenaded by a symphony of angels, and a resurrection — striking in a boldness of color and form that seems to anticipate the much later artworks of William Blake. These panels, hanging like doors, were swung on their hinges and opened up at the appropriate liturgical seasons, covering up the crucifixion panel. The crucifixion was thus enframed by both ends of the Paschal Mystery: the incarnation of the Logos-Son in the flesh of Jesus, and the resurrection of the crucified Lord. If we could imagine ourselves as patients gazing on Grünewald's crucifixion, we might find ourselves focusing on the reality of our diseased state, and, perhaps, during other times of year when those other panels were on display, on the whole of life in which our suffering appears, from the joy of our birth to the hope in risen life.

One lesson to be derived from the Grünewald altarpiece is that while the cross does not allow for an imaginary escape from suffering, neither does it consign human beings to a life of hopelessness. Rather it turns the viewer toward a wider reality, an imaginative world within which present suffering is taking place. This can lead to a sense of hope planted firmly in the reality of the present condition, facing it and going through it. It is in *going through* that one finds where God stands in relation to human suffering. A Christian imagination is not a leap into an alternate fantasy world, but rather a way of seeing that can only be gained by entering into the agony of the flesh.

The Christic Imagination

Facing reality, going through it, suffering it, and entering into a region of hope: this is, in a different way, also the approach to the problem of dark suffering found in the thought of William Lynch. Lynch was a Jesuit of prolific imagination and, judging from his writings, of unusual insight into the human condition. Trained in the classics, he wrote on the complex interrelationships between poetry, drama and faith. He was one of the earliest Catholic writers to take the arts seriously, not only literature and drama, but also film. His work is a cross-section of classical erudition, literary analysis, cultural theory, philosophy, theology, and psychology.[3]

Lynch was friend and colleague to many estimable artists and writers who helped him shape his own thinking on and explorations into what he would call the "Christic" imagination, which stresses the form and person of Christ in the shaping of faith and religious imagination. While serving for several years as editor of *Thought*, the prestigious journal of arts and letters once published at Fordham University, he developed this "Christic" key to the rest of his work. Most notable in this development are a series of three articles on theology and imagination published in 1954 and 1955.[4] The Christic imagination is shaped by and reflective of the central mystery of Christ, which is that contact with the infinite that comes through the finite. The key to understanding human life, including suffering, is entering into the "mysteries of Christ."[5] In these articles Lynch tries to move theology away from its more abstracted intellectualist forms to something different: an exercise of imagination imbued with the mystery of Christ, which means an imagination rooted in the concrete reality of the Word-made-*flesh*. Far from indulging in fantasy, the task of the imagination is to make present to the mind what is real, just as Christian faith holds that the incarnation makes present to human consciousness both the full reality of God and of human nature. In *Images of Hope*, he would write that the imagination is " . . . that total set of forces in man which contributes to the formation of the full contextual image of an object."[6] It is so bound up with wishing, the often subconscious formation of desires, "that it is inalienable to what it means to be human; without it, the human lapses into boredom, acedia, depression and hopelessness."

The Christ-imbued, or "Christic," imagination, then, is radically incarnationalist. It takes as its starting point the human matter and world in which God chose to reveal himself, and in which, according to Christian faith, God chose to dwell, of which God became a part. As classical Christological doctrine boldly asserts, the finite has been penetrated and assumed by the divine, in the form of a finite body, even unto and including death. Christology is therefore belief in the capacity of the actual to reveal the divine, that "if we imagine and live through it [human existence as it is]," it will "lead somewhere."[7] He describes this "Christic" impulse in rather masculine terms as "athletic" and "penetrating" and "energizing" of the poetic imagination as well as the life of faith, relying here on ancient metaphors for the entry of the Word into the flesh.[8]

But this Christic imagination calls for bearing with complexity, even relishing the ambiguity that attends an ongoing process of seeing things in new ways. The Christic imagination is not "magical" but, as Thomas Aquinas explained, works through "participation" and by way of analogy.[9] It is flexible and non-rigid;[10] not simply analytical, treating of ideas in abstraction, but also historical and open to the flow of narrative, story and myth.[11] Like reality itself, it resists reduction to a simplistic formulation, to a single point of view. In fact, the Christic imagination poses a challenge to any tendency to settle for the literalistic and uncontemplated, much less the apodictic and absolutist. Lynch calls this latter form of imagination *univocal*, allowing for but one voice. It is countered by what he terms the *analogical* imagination, which opens us to a pluralism of experiences and possible understandings of reality.[12]

The analogical imagination deals with the uneven fits between those things that are similar to each other, but not necessarily exactly the same or representing the same reality.[13] Christ is like Apollo or Krishna or Buddha, but also decidedly different, not only as a historical personage, but in who he is and what he represents, as both mythologically and theologically understood. The analogical imagination can therefore deal with ambiguity, and embrace that ambiguity as a principle of life. This is crucial for seeing that not all forms of spiritual consolation are necessarily valid or even authentic responses to suffering, nor all forms of suffering equal expressions of the mystery of evil in the world. For example, some suffering may simply be the result of human stupidity, arrogance, or hubris. A sense of ambiguity, and acceptance of it, leads to a balance in the Christian imagination, as, for example, between the tragic, on the one hand, and the comic, on the other.[14]

Here Lynch is dipping into his extensive mastery of the classical drama, and attempting to show that, for the Christian imagination, life is marked by both the radical disjuncture symbolized by the tragedy of the cross, and also by resolutions and finalities (as realized in classical comedy), contained in the resurrection.[15] While confronting the tragic, Christian imagination retains a horizon rooted in the comic, which is marked by a deep sense of the ultimate over-coming of and resolution of the tragic. Comedy, Lynch asserts, does not allow us to forget that we are human.[16] It is the "enemy of the uni-vocal mind."[17] It is opposed to "Manichaean" views that would pit the Christian approach to reality against reality itself, Christ against culture, or Christian optimism over and against real tragedy, as though because there is suffering in the world, the world is therefore to be shunned or spurned. The evasion of the comic in the form of literalism or escapism is the trap of small minds and typically expresses itself theologically in an unfortunate doctrinal narrowness. For " ... both the poet and the saint are agreed that the be-all and end-all of life is the liberation of the imagination, as the sign of decay and death is its fixities and rigidities."[18] But theological myopia or dogmatism most fears that moment when the clear and distinct idea begins to diffract, like the colors of a prism, into many other ideas of different hues. The univocal imagination is tantamount to " ... the fundamental fear of entrance, of birth, of movement into the world, of 'happening.' For with it [i.e., birth, movement into the world] begins this diffractive process."[19] Freed from such fear, the analogical imagination revels in

48

a sense of irony about life — a sense that life is neither wholly tragic nor wholly comic, but rather something that is lived "in between" these extremes, often enough swinging back and forth between them.

The univocal imagination, on the other hand, tends toward a Manichaeism bereft of the flexibility and suppleness of an analogical approach. The great cultural as well as religious divides of our time, as well as of other times, derive "from a loss of faith in the limited image or thing, from a lack of patience for the staying with it as a path to the infinite. We stalwartly refuse the kind of intricate, associating act between the two (finite and infinite) which is the vocation of the analogical act."[20] This refusal to engage reality as it is leads to what Lynch calls the "absolutizing instinct," in the form of rebellion against the world (through heroic or romantic evasions of the tragic), dissociation (in the form of polarizations and escapes into false mysticism or magic), or flight from it into various forms of what Lynch calls "angelism" or denial of the body.[21] A Christian imagination lacking a sense of irony about life as it is can become a rather dour thing, the ally of narrow-mindedness and bigotry, and certainly one that shuns embodied reality.

What this means is that the Christian imagination will not indulge in idealist alternatives to what reality itself presents. The "finite concrete is the only healthy path to the goal of the imagination."[22] Christian imagination does not engage in a denial of suffering, but in a forthright encounter with it, for purposes of letting the work of Christian faith be accomplished. Of course, encounter with the real, things as they concretely are, can be crushing. This is why Lynch calls for a rediscovery of the "natural" symbol, most essentially that of the body, which does not divert us from actuality through an act of transcendence or theorizing about some reality beyond what is *in concreto*. This is why he can say of Proust that there is in his writing " . . . no theory of a deeper entrance into the actual, into the daylight world, in order to tie down a surer dream."[23] When Marcel bites into that famous madeleine in *Swann's Way* and savors its buttery flavor, we find a reciprocal relationship between reality and the subject, a relationship mediated by the symbol[24] of his eating, taking into himself the outside world, and sensing it in and through his body, beginning with the taste buds on his tongue. This is base-line realism, directly tied to the body.

Lynch could well have appreciated Grünewald's crucifixion for similar reasons. The representation of the body of Jesus there allows for no evasion of the real. But in our age, he argues, the symbol, especially the natural symbol of the body, has lost this power, and is fundamentally uninterested in the actual.[25] In our time (quite a few years after Lynch) the body has become an abstraction, an ideal to be realized through "sculpting" and surgery and injections. Beyond the body, we might look at the "symbol" of the flag. The flag points us toward an ideal world, perhaps a fiction, which, bathed in romantic feeling, does not necessarily evoke reality, but often only an alternative to the reality we know, under the banner of "patriotism" or loyalty. Or, it can evoke a set of ideals, even ideas, that are not yet fully realized. (The swastika had such compelling power for many during the Nazi regime.)[26] In any case, symbols so construed lead us back into a split world where the symbol, as ideal form, be it body or flag or cross, stands over and against concrete reality itself as an unattainable ideal.

Yet this is the very outcome that Lynch's Christic imagination works against. The body of Christ is not an ideal body; it is utterly real. The natural symbol of the body could not be more boldly at work than it is in the Christian revelation, from the incarnation through the crucifixion and in the resurrection. The symbol of the cross, then, is not to be understood as evoking a particular theology, nor even a spirituality, much less a religious ideology of suffering. It is rather the historical point of mediation among human beings who suffer, and the reality of suffering entered into by God in the form of a body.

In facing suffering, therefore, the Christian imagination is incarnational in its foundation and direction rather than idealistic; it is ironic rather than literal, much less blithely optimistic. And it is mediated analogically in and through those central symbols of Christian faith that evoke the Christic fact that the infinite, the sacred, is found within the human. For Christian imagination, the sacred is reached only in and through a penetration of the finite, the real, within embodied existence in the world. All this insight is contained in the symbol of the cross itself.

When the cross is understood as the concrete embodiment of the divine entrance into the real, it can serve as a foundation for hope. From the human side of the ledger, hope comes from an insertion into the world and a penetration of the real that will eventually lead to an encounter with the infinite, with God. Yet it is important to understand that Lynch is not arguing as a theologian, in which case he would be careful to suggest that hope is itself a gift of God, a *theo*logical virtue. Although his own imagination is theologically informed and profoundly so, his focus is on the human, the human condition for the possibility of arriving at hope in life. This is why he stresses the imagination so much: that part of human existence which, theologically speaking, cooperates with God's grace and works to lead us out of hopelessness, not via any escape routes or detours around suffering, but by envisioning ways to go through it.

Moving through the Real

Lynch's work on imagination was deepened by his passing through a period of hopelessness during his own hospitalization for exhaustion and depression.[27] Indeed, he is perhaps most widely known and remembered for *Images of Hope*, first published in 1962, written in the wake of his own ordeal. With no direct advertence to himself or his experience, he nevertheless wrote a book that was then groundbreaking in its intelligent embrace of psychotherapy, a rather unusual move in Catholic circles of the time.[28] But more significant were the descriptions within the book of the experience of what he termed mental illness, of the despair to which it often leads, and the utter helplessness sensed by a person so afflicted. The book is itself a kind of phenomenology of suffering, and of the path out of it, through the exercise of imagination, and with help coming from outside the imprisonment within, or what he calls entrapment by, dark suffering. But here again he does not refer to a "Christian" imagination per se, but rather to what is more fundamental and what is revealed in the

Christian imagination, the Christic event: the depths and powers of the *human* for arriving at hope:

> What we ought especially to do together is to study the content of the human with the help of "the human imagination." That is to say, together we must imagine the nature and the range of the human, until we come to include more and more of the human forms of illness, in increasingly satisfactory ways, under the noble word *human*.[29]

As we have already noted, Lynch believed that it is by driving into the heart of human actuality, finitude, that one arrives at a sense of the transcendent depths of the human, and ultimately, at hope. Focusing on the pain of those who suffer from "mental illness," such as severe depression, he found "hope" for many people to be at best a "hoping against hope," the search for a future of some kind not yet visible, not yet imaginable, and hence quite possibly an expression of despair.[30] Mental illness is characterized by a hopelessness that derives from a constriction of the human imagination to see beyond the prison walls of disease. The ability to "wish" is eviscerated by the disease itself. The afflicted person cannot even know his deepest wishes because the imagination is not enlivened to its own possibilities, much less to a world beyond. It is as if the Isenheim altarpiece consisted only of the horror of the crucifixion, with no nativity or resurrection. The result can be a sense of entrapment, impossibility, ultimately leading to apathy (*a-patheia*), the absence of any affect.[31]

As Simone Weil, Susan Sontag, and others have attested, these feelings can only deepen when one finds oneself within the realm of those who deem themselves to be "well." Such, we may infer, was the situation, in broad terms, in which Lynch found himself at one time in his life. *Images of Hope* is therefore a way of describing the journey from suffering in hopelessness to freedom in a new-found sense of hope through a recovery of the powers of imagination. All of this presumes and takes place within the ambit of the Christic paradigm which prizes the priority of penetrating the real in order to go through it and to arrive at hope, based on the pattern of God's entrance into the human in and through Christ.

How does Lynch proceed to do this? *Images of Hope* is divided into three parts. Part One is a description of hopelessness as an integral dimension of mental illness, and of the structure and forms that hope would take in the face of the experience of hopelessness. Part Two discusses the psychological dimensions of hope in relation to wishing, and the psychic forms and dynamisms of the movement toward hope. This is in many ways the central part of the author's argument, how to enable in the unwell the capacity for exercising the imagination, or of "wishing" in the Freudian sense of seeing and naming in symbolic ways one's deepest unconscious desires for a way out of psychological darkness. Part Three looks at hope as a metaphysical reality, not merely an assertion of will, a forced hope against hope, but rather a reality based upon the power of analogy, opening a person up to a world of possibility, precisely through noting similarities and differences between oneself and others, and welcoming both ambiguity and a sense of irony, as well as of the comic aspects of life as we find it. My focus here will be on the first part, because that is where Lynch lays the foundation for everything else, and where his work fits most helpfully into the overall project of this book: that a Christian response to suffering must include the cross, but must also expand the context within which the cross is understood and encountered.

Hope itself is a relative idea: it is imbedded in life's contexts. It lives "in a field of life"[32] where the limitations of the present do not seem absolute, no longer quite the imprisonment one had always thought. A door suddenly swings open, a wall gives way. One could walk out if one only knew what to wish for, to imagine, to "see" as lying on the other side. For the ill, it could denote the means by which one regains health; for the hungry, satisfaction; for the war-torn, a cessation of bombing: "solutions" that are, at one point, beyond the point of imagining. In all cases, it requires a recovery of some sense of a world beyond one's own suffering, of an "outside world" that can be re-entered, or entered into for the first time, with the help of someone who cares. An outside world represents a "way out" and some sense of possibility.[33]

Hope is thus not an "emergency virtue" that would paper over the muck of life.[34] Nor does it suggest merely transcending difficulties, escaping imprisonments through various escapist schemes or by succumbing to the desire for absolutes.[35] For all of these can be forms of denial of reality, and reality cannot be dealt with except by going through it.[36] Hope, therefore, is born in part of an act of imagination, envisioning what cannot yet be seen. As such it is an inner resource, linked, as a sense of comedy is, with an ironic acceptance of the ordinary, even if that ordinary is a convoluted and conflicted reality.[37]

Hope begins with the "help" of finding a way of standing outside oneself, if one can. But, at the same time, it is not a matter of self-help, as if the answer to suffering somehow comes only from within — following the familiar bromide that "God helps those who help themselves." Hope depends, first, on the offer of help, and the mutual recognition that we depend on one another in life-giving ways. In the Isenheim altarpiece, this is poignantly depicted in the hands of Mary, clenched in anguish at the foot of the cross, the consoling hand of John the Beloved Disciple grasping her arm and holding her up. This sense of mutual support, sharing in suffering — what Jon Sobrino and Dorothee Sölle and others would later call "solidarity" — is born, first, from the inward act of taking help — not simply passively accepting it, but of appropriating it, making it somehow a part of oneself. This is the only way we can face and go through reality, as part of a dynamic response to reality and the suffering it entails. We could not hope without help, but help alone, as unappropriated offer, will not facilitate our penetration into the reality of our own lives. Solidarity depends upon acceptance of solidarity, the solidarity of others with us. Something of this insight is certainly at work in the process of psychoanalysis, where the analysand must undertake an active effort to work at appropriating the "help" that comes in the process and through the mediation of the analyst. So, too, in more ordinary and everyday human settings. And this calls for an exercise of imagination, of putting things together in order to be able to see in new ways.

Hopelessness, on the other hand, is the result of either an absence of help, hence of the possibility for this inner dynamism of the imagination to envision what cannot yet be seen, or of a failure to appropriate help in whatever form it is offered and made present. The outcome is an inability to face what is real because of a prior sense of impossibility. There is the sense that there are no resources, outer or inner, to call upon.[38] One feels overwhelmed and all seems futile: "The striving self cannot reach the ideal self: hope is destroyed."[39]

As we noted in the chapter 1, Lynch clearly does not wish to suggest that such situations of hopelessness are illusory. A sense of hopelessness may become a reality for many people, at least at some point in their lives.[40] And the real outside world often enough does not in fact offer the help that is needed, but instead communicates the message that one's help must come from within. In the face of this depth of imprisonment, one really is left to oneself, and must, at some point, either succumb to despair, or somehow "choose life,"[41] even if it makes no sense to do so, even if it means simply dying thus entrapped. But to claim oneself as a human person, even in the terror of entrapment, is the beginning of hope, a matter of claiming one's "right" as a human being vis-à-vis a sickness that has no rights. Entrapped by a disease, one desires to be a full member of the human family.

This is not hoping against hope; it is a claiming of oneself over and against the suffering of disease. The real fantasy is to hold that my disease is who I am. Such is no more the case than saying that the blue lesions on Christ's body are Christ himself. Yes, the disease has its reality, but I am no longer an unimaginable ideal: I am a human being, flesh and blood, even more real than the disease that afflicts me. Lynch elaborates:

> ... [T]he sick person has the right and the need to conceive
> of himself as human and as permitted to act positively and
> creatively. The sickness is at every moment a real sickness and
> very painful, but in itself it is a fantasy, a fantasy image of the
> self, which leads to thoughts, feelings, actions. This image may
> be absolutely preoccupying and intense, but it is still and for all

that a lie, without rights. To say that we must get well before we deal with this image is to put the cart before the horse. The illness has no rights.[42]

The image of self as sickness itself has to be replaced with an image of self that generates hope. Lynch asks whether various people deemed ill "have the right to hold their heads up in pride and dignity." The answer is that they definitely do:

Not because of what they seem to themselves to be at the moment, and upon which they act, but because of what they really are and do not yet see. (Hope acts in the name of what is not yet seen.) They are human and can love; everybody can. But some do not give themselves the right to be human, or have had the right taken away from them by others.[43]

We are all in the dark, we are all suffering, we are all in need of help.

In our darkness there are many other points that can conquer the endless. These points will emerge with greater clarity if the darkness is seen as common to the sick and the well, and not seen patronizingly from the outside, from the glory of our hygienic, microbe-free light.[44]

Lynch is saying that we all need to exercise our imaginations in order to "see" an outside world, whether we are in fact in the grip of illness or not. More to the point: we all need to discover the fundamental image of hope, which is the human being itself. What Lynch does not say explicitly here, but what is hanging in the background of the entire project, is a theological conviction that this *humanum* is made known in all its aspects in the full mystery of Christ, from incarnation through the cross and resurrection — all that is contained within the Christic imagination.

However, the new self and world that we imagine must belong not to an ideal world, but only to the real. The alternative is an absolute ideal — of goodness or purity or holiness or health — that may have nothing to do with the flesh and blood existence of human beings. What Lynch calls the "absolutizing instinct" is the enemy of the human and of hope, leading to a world of false hope,[45] and investing certain aspects of life, especially the moment of death, with an importance disproportionate to their actual weight in the whole of a life.[46] The result can be an exacerbation of the suffering that already exists. In religious categories, this absolutizing instinct can result in calculated theologies, ranging from theories of retribution rebutted in the Book of Job, to the theodicies of the Enlightenment period (discussed in chapter 3), that would calibrate the relations between God and humankind so precisely as to reduce them to rational categories.[47] The absolutizing instinct would therefore drive us further away from the real and more toward an ideal of both who we are and who God is in relation to us. We could well end up establishing false gods: personal power, wealth, prestige, repressive political ideologies, and dangerously selective forms of religion. Yet, for Lynch, the "entire good" of religion is to fight the absolutizing instinct. Religions ought to teach people to be able to live in waiting, in ambiguity, in something less than the full light of day.[48] "If, therefore, we really wish to imitate God, let us make men free."[49]

The road to freedom, however, is an arduous one. To be freed of absolutes, whether we are "sick" or "well," calls for "a new interior ability to handle ambiguities." Giving these up, and in a sense being born again, is initially agonizing, an experience of suffering in itself. For this involves giving up, losing many hopes, albeit "false" ones, in order to be freed of hopelessness. One must walk through the fire in order to reach the golden apples.[50] One is reminded here of the harrowing passage of Papageno in Mozart's "Magic Flute," which is itself an echo of the passage of Orpheus:

> To move through the fire into the valley of the human is to move right through the whole camp of these absolutes. Everything the self turns to for salvation actually dissolves and gives no grip upon itself. Everything is at first a fire, yet it turns out to be not fire but a balm.... To give up an "absolute," to give up a "necessity," to give up that with which one is absolutely identified, to give up what was a point of absolute security, to give up a black-and-white world — each of the surrenders is

a trial by fire. But each turns out to be a balm because these things were weights that burdened us and brought no taste of freedom.[51]

As we have noted, this requires facing the reality of suffering, going through it. Letting go of false absolutes and hopelessness can only be accomplished by the harrowing of a trial, as by fire. To be in the midst of that fire is to invite a new experience of confusion and hopelessness, though no longer of imprisonment or entrapment.

Miller's Geography of Crisis

How does one give up that black-and-white world to which Lynch refers? Lynch's radical realism allows for no avoiding what is revealed either about suffering or about hope in the symbol of the cross. But it should also be obvious that the cross does not, cannot, stand alone in the Christian imagination. To do so would be to absolutize one dimension of the revelation of God in Jesus Christ — a crucial one, to be sure, but one that gives us only part of the picture. For Lynch, the prior principle governing a Christian imagination is the incarnation, the entry of God into a world of human suffering, God's offer of "help" to the suffering. The cross, seen in this light, becomes an expression of where suffering leads, and also of where love is drawn. At the same time, the cross becomes a locus of hope, not in spite of what is going on there, but because it occasions the great exercise of Christian imagination: a dissolution of the walls of imprisonment, a movement through but beyond death, and a release into a new outer world. However, this exercise of hope, this living in hope, is not reached by an avoidance of suffering, but rather by facing it, going through it, taking stock of the points where, as in the Isenheim altarpiece, the flesh meets the wood, where the nails penetrate the flesh.[52] But how does one get there? How does one learn from suffering by facing it, when all our instincts would point to the wisdom of avoiding it in the interest of self-preservation and freedom from pain? Whereas Lynch took the affliction of mental illness as his prime example, the philosopher Jerome A. Miller looks at the dynamics of tragic reversal

58

and peels away the layers of self-defense that stand in the way of facing terrible darkness.

In his book, *The Way of Suffering*, Miller begins with a shocking image: a father walks into the bedroom of his teenage son and discovers to his horror and disbelief that his son has hanged himself from the ceiling. The father learns that, unbeknownst to him, his son was gay. Later he learns that his son had been unable, indeed was terrified, to share this fact even with a father who was, by all measures, loving and generous. The discovery of his dead son, a tragic reversal in the trajectory of an otherwise flourishing life, precipitates a crisis in the father. This tragedy forces the question of whether he will face the horrific reality of what has happened and the truth about his son and himself that it possibly harbors, or whether he will turn away from it in fear of what he cannot bring himself to face, that which fills him with dread. The problem, as Miller describes it, is that

> [w]e are, far more than we can bear to admit, the prisoners of our own avoidances.... If the will to control originates in my desire to protect myself from something devastating, the only way to become truly receptive to the world is to open myself to that devastating experience and do nothing to interfere with it. The only way to stop avoiding is to suffer.... For radical transformation cannot be brought about through one's accomplishing it, but only through one's suffering of it. It is not something I can *do*, but rather something occurs by virtue of my being wholly *undone*, by virtue of my succumbing to my own disintegration....[53]

The father recognizes, however, that he cannot finally avoid the dreadful gravity of what has happened — this, his reality — and that its bearing down upon him will require an existential obedience, a submission to the fact and force of his son's death and to the life and circumstances that gave rise to it. How could he have missed what was happening to his son? How could he have been so unknowing of himself? He sees that the sheer fact of his son's suicide has forced upon him a question of his openness to a world that will inevitably shatter his old one, and that this very openness will of necessity lead to the suffering of further loss.

> His world is ended, just as surely as it would be if the noose were wound around his own neck.... The dead body of his son is flesh of his flesh and, at the same time, the very incarnation of something horrifying and totally foreign to him. It is the one thing in the universe he cannot embrace without being totally shattered.[54]

But he also knows that only by surrendering to and going through this very suffering can he reach the new world of wisdom that is, in this tragedy, his destination and newly discovered vocation:

> The only real alternative to all these avoidances is to let crisis uproot one's life, to obey its unsettling summons with no reservations. To do this requires that one allow suffering's unpredictable and pitiless demands to impinge on one's life at every moment. One promises to follow dread where it leads, even if this costs not less than everything. But in doing so, one converts one's exile, one's homelessness, into a pilgrimage on behalf of dread's dark and elusive truths; one becomes the pupil of its harrowing lessons.[55]

Thus begins the journey. It begins with the "end of the world" as the father once knew it. At this juncture he faces the "rupture of devastation" as he engages in a struggle with a lingering "will to control" that will not let him face the heart of his suffering. Yet it is only when he realizes that the old world is now completely gone, and that he cannot will it into some semblance of a continuing, unruffled existence, that he can face this tragedy as a crisis, as a point of decision rather than only as a point of temporary setback. For the old world has indeed imploded with the death of his son. He now understands that not only has his own life been changed, but that somehow, mysteriously, because his life was caught up in his son's, he cannot avoid facing what led to his son's demise. It is now becoming clearer that his life up to this moment has been a massive exercise in evading the truth to be gleaned from the reality of his life. He must face the fact that he might have missed something, in spite of or perhaps precisely because of his goodness. He must face the fact that he is horrified in the face of this death. He is in the midst of what Miller calls here the "throes of tragic reversal."[56]

From this point onward the father faces a series of passages in which his defenses are stripped away, one by one. He realizes that, in contrast to fear and terror, the dread he feels in the face of this reality is actually the dread of surrender, of the heart's consent to go through what must be gone through in order to reach the freedom of the truth. Dread can lead to paralysis, and thus to hopelessness, or it can lead, through the heart's consent, to an obedience to what horrifies.[57] The sense of "obedience" here is different than in the sense suggested by Simone Weil. This is not a passive submission to the blind and mechanical force of fate, an *islam,* as though we were merely matter subjected to the laws of gravity. It is rather a response to what summons us, stirring us from our slumber, even as we move against contrary inclinations of dread and the inertia generated by psychic and spiritual pain. It is a surrender, the beginning of a pilgrimage toward the sacred. This pilgrimage ultimately leads, as does every authentic pilgrimage that is not just a diversion or a prolonged vacation, to a position of "prostration" before the sacred, and a "death-like birth" into a new stance in life. Here we are on territory not unlike that of Job before the whirlwind.

In the course of his pilgrimage into the truth, the father in Miller's parable learns three hard-won lessons — wisdom come against his will.

First, he is up against a transcendent "Other" that meets him in the awesome force of this tragic reversal, what Miller later identifies as the power of the gods, or the sacred. He has managed until the time of this event to avoid facing what always threatened to disrupt his orderly and even exemplary life: the sacred itself. He realizes that refusing the sacred entry into his life now would be refusing the sacred altogether. Although he has fancied himself to be quite open to the sacred, even generous in his embrace of it through a welcoming way of life, he has perhaps underestimated the power of the sacred to disrupt, and has perhaps confused his "domestic gods" with a holy Other that is in fact threatening to the established order.

Therefore, Miller writes, "... we retract our gesture of welcome at the very moment when we realize we have offered it to a reality that has the capacity to wound us mortally."[58]

Second, he learns that genuine openness to this transcendent Other, the sacred, comes through a frank surrender to the darkness that has enveloped him in his grief. Yet grief changes the face of God. God turns out not to be as familiar as he had once thought, or as religious institutions and their rituals and customs and pieties had made God out to be. The divine powers now threaten him with an overwhelming claim that is both dreadful and inescapable. Transcendence now receives a new shade of meaning: it the divine visitation that arrives as an acquaintance with powerlessness in the face of suffering, an insight beautifully captured in Second Isaiah: "He was spurned and avoided by men, a man of suffering, accustomed to infirmity, One of those from whom men hide their faces, spurned, and we held him in no esteem" (Isa. 53:30).

Third, this encounter with suffering through tragedy leads finally to a merciless confrontation of the father with himself. He must face the threat of the dissolution of his old self, his old world, and his sense of bearing within it. Horror in the face of the evil of suffering and death takes on a moral character, forcing upon him a consideration of what he has unwittingly wrought. The father in this parable is forced to look not only at the fact that he has become a stranger to himself, but also at the collapsed world that he and his family and his son had inhabited for so many years. In this moment of transcendence the father finally admits that although the meaning of his life is unfathomable, out of his confusion he finds a new degree of freedom to respond to the sacred within a newly constituted reality. His former self is dead, and a new self has emerged, risen from the dead, as it were.

From the standpoint of faith, the father in this parable has all along been engaged in an encounter with the cross in his life. This encounter has involved the wound of tragic reversal, a radical re-imagining of God, and the stripping away of old self and old world that are required for a new image to take shape. The pattern of the cross is kenotic, self-dispossessing. It leads into a pattern of life that entails familiarity with suffering, even without comprehending it, and ultimately, the courage to look into the faces of others in their suffering reality and not to turn away. As St. John of the Cross suggested in the *Dark Night*, those who have everything taken from them, through death, tragedy, calamity, or spiritual trial, are, ironically, those who, even in their darkness, can finally find themselves most secure in God.[59] In the darkness of existence, one reaches the threshold either of hope or despair, two experiences which are, as Lynch has noted, intrinsically related in their dancing on the precipice of hopelessness.[60]

The human spirit is liberated to the degree that it faces the various forms that evil assumes, thus rendering itself open to the sacred. Such an encounter with the sacred can only occur through an acquaintance with the suffering experienced in the dreadful encounters with human existence that are simply forced upon us against our wills. Hope lies in going through that suffering and only thereby arriving at new images of life.

Part Two

God and the
Crosses of Suffering

Chapter Three

Searching for God

Oh in childhood, God, how easy you were:
you, whom I cannot take hold of now, anywhere.
One smiled on the things one loved to have around;
they came half way: and you were already in reach.
And now, my God, where should I travel to find you?
Where do I enter? What mountain must I climb?
If someone asks for you: where should I point?
Where is your rustling grove? Where does your animal wander?[1]

— Rainer Maria Rilke

At least since the appearance of *The Imitation of Christ* in the early fifteenth century, the classic Christian response to the magnitude of suffering has been to offer the cross as path of union with the sufferings of Jesus.[2] The advice offered in the *Imitation* is directed toward all Christians: "Everything is founded on the cross and everything depends on our dying on the cross. There is no other way to life and interior peace except the holy way of the cross and our daily dying to self." The one who hangs on the gallows is one who pierces our own hearts with a recognition of how senseless suffering is, how abhorrent to God, and yet how mysteriously close it draws us to a God who otherwise seems quite distant from us in the midst of our own sufferings and those of the world.

Searching for God on the Cross

In the wake of the Holocaust, the Bomb, and the "irruption of the poor"[3] in history, Christian theologians such as Jürgen Moltmann and Jon Sobrino have mined the symbol of the cross not only for its pertinence to the suffering that has descended upon whole peoples, as well as individual persons, but for something more fundamental: Where God stands in relation to suffering. For Moltmann, the cross is the site of God's direct entry into the realm of human suffering. The Trinitarian relations, especially between the Father and the Son, are revealed in the cross itself, for in the sufferings of Jesus, God the Father himself suffers. The *kenosis* of Philippians 2, which Moltmann lyrically describes as "the final and complete self-humiliation of God in man and in the person of Jesus,"[4] is the participation of God in human suffering. On the cross, then, the "incarnate God is present," to every human being who suffers, and draws near to everyone who is forsaken. "There is no loneliness and no rejection which he has not taken to himself and assumed in the Cross of Jesus."[5]

While not a direct reference to the cross of Jesus, Elie Wiesel's famous recounting of the hanging of the young boy at Auschwitz evokes all of this sense of God's manifestation in the execution of the innocent victim by the powers of evil. The adult prisoners were forced to watch as the boy was hanged in front of them, and were then forced to file by him and gaze upon his death agony:

> For more than half an hour he stayed there, struggling between life and death, dying in slow agony under our eyes. And we had to look him full in the face. He was still alive when I passed in front of him. His tongue was still red, his eyes were not yet glazed.
> Behind me, I heard the same man asking:
> "Where is God now?"
> And I heard a voice within me answer him:
> "Where is He? Here He is — He is hanging here on this gallows...."[6]

Like Wiesel, writing in the wake of the Holocaust, Moltmann concludes that "like the cross of Christ, even Auschwitz is in God himself. Even Auschwitz is taken up into the grief of the Father, the surrender of the Son, and the power of the Spirit."[7] This is true because the crucified God is also in all the Auschwitzes of the world. "Christian faith does not believe in a new 'idea' of God. In the fellowship of the crucified Christ it finds itself in a new 'situation of God' and participates in that with all its existence."[8] The cross is the real symbol of God's participation in our sufferings, and of the placement of our sufferings in the suffering of God. Human beings, in their sufferings, thus participate really in the suffering of God for us, and enter into a kind of *theosis*, or divinization. (I will discuss in chapter 4 Rahner's reservations about claiming such a direct involvement of God in human suffering.)

While Sobrino shares much of Moltmann's view of the world as a place of the cross, he prefers to speak of the Crucified God only in light of the sufferings of "Crucified People" of history. What characterizes the scandal of the cross is the "radical discontinuity" between the mode of Jesus' death and the relationship with his Father. For what he confronts, and what we confront, on the cross, is the seeming absence of God in his absolute silence in the face of Jesus' suffering.[9] What is revealed here, as in the sufferings of the poor and oppressed, is "the immense power of the anti-Kingdom triumphing over the Kingdom."[10] "The cross therefore raises the most serious problem, whether and how not acting, not speaking, how silence, withdrawal, inaction can reveal anything of God."[11] Yet, for Sobrino, God's silence becomes a paradoxical expression of God's solidarity with the victims of history in their powerlessness:

> There is no recipe for recognizing God on the cross, and initially there is nothing on the cross but silence and scandal. If in faith, however, we accept that God is there, then we have to be ready for the great surprise that God is not as we think. We have to be ready to find God not only through the positive, but also through the negative. We have to be ready to see God, not only as the greater God, but also as the lesser God....[12]

And why should this be the case? Because only then can we see God as a God of solidarity with those who suffer, and only then can we help "to bring the crucified down from their crosses" in our own solidarity with those who suffer.[13]

Other theologians, most especially Sölle and Schillebeeckx, have warned against an emphasis on the cross that derogates from the full message of hope that is partially revealed there, but also in so much more of Christian revelation. Their concern, certainly shared by Sobrino and other liberation theologians, as well as by some feminist theologians, is that isolation of the cross can lead to a spirituality of masochism and passive acceptance of certain forms of suffering, such as the misery following upon economic and social injustice, the sources of which must be challenged. In her elegant book simply entitled *Suffering*, Sölle moves toward a theology of the cross by first describing the multidimensional character of human suffering in a modern European situation. She relies on an extensive quotation from a German factory worker who describes the depths of his suffering as he works long hours under extremely difficult physical conditions, the sense of imprisonment and social isolation that are exacted of him, and the resultant sense of despondency and resignation to fate that he faces.[14] His suffering finally leads him to the brink of despair: "Believe me! More and more often I get the feeling that they're soon going to throw me away like an old rag. In fact I'm afraid that soon no one will know me, neither the foreman nor my children. Folks, what's left for me to believe in?"[15]

Several factors about suffering come to light here: its dark and multifaceted character, including spiritual suffering; the sense of imprisonment by fate or destiny to which it leads; a sense of the meaninglessness of life and worthlessness of self; and a warping sense of time — a sense of being out-of-time, waiting for reprieve, not believing it will ever come.[16] All the while, the one who suffers yearns to scream, but cannot; one waits for the scream to surge forth, for "[t]he scream of suffering contains all the despair of which a person is capable, and in this sense every scream is a scream for God."[17]

God is indeed the problem that suffering raises for faith and for theology. In suffering, we face the potential for a real crisis of faith. But even before we might turn to the arguments of a theodicy, the justification of God's goodness before suffering and evil, God is a problem in a more immediately religious sense: God seems to require of his creatures a life of suffering. Submission to it becomes for some a spiritual ideal.[18] Even worse, God looks like a sadist, one who not only allows and requires his creatures to suffer, but who sends them suffering, demanding of them the impossible.[19] This leads to a view of God who is either insensitive to human misery, or who is simply brutal.[20] As Sölle sees it, theodicy is called into question because God is called into question even before we construct a theodicy. The answer to the famous question posed in Wiesel's *Night*, "Where is God now?" has another chilling and tempting answer: God doesn't care — an answer not far removed from Sobrino's starting point: a God of chilling silence.

Despite the value of her contribution to religious thought about suffering, this seems to be near the position of Simone Weil. In her stunning essay, "The 'Iliad,' Poem of Might," she says that sheer might, or force, bears down upon the sufferer in unimaginable ways. While this is a great anti-war essay, it can also be read as a development of her thoughts on affliction in general:

> Might is that which makes a thing of anybody who comes under its sway. When exercised to the full, it makes a thing of man in the most literal sense, for it makes him a corpse. There where someone stood a moment ago, stands no one.... From the power to transform him into a thing by killing him there proceeds another power, and much more prodigious, that which makes a thing of him while he still lives. He is living, he has a soul, yet he is a thing. A strange being is that thing which has a soul, and strange the state of that soul. Who knows how often during each instant it must torture and destroy itself in order to conform? The soul was not made to dwell in a thing; and when forced to it, there is no part of that soul but suffers violence.[21]

The only possible Christian response to such severe suffering is therefore obedience to the mechanisms of necessity over which we have no control yet through which God works a loving will. Just as the seas obey the laws of physics, so one who suffers affliction must assume the docility of matter. In this obedience, she argues elsewhere, the grace of God comes and possesses us, and we discover what is meant by joy.[22] "Affliction is therefore a marvel of divine technique"[23] to which one must simply submit, even as God remains silent.

Understandable as this bleak conclusion may be from the standpoint of so much human experience, it is finally unacceptable from the standpoint of Christian faith. In Sölle's account, resignation to such a conclusion amounts to masochism, realized at best as a quasi-Stoic mute endurance of what cannot be changed.[24] This, in turn, leads to self-isolation, an inability to communicate what is lodged most deeply in one's heart, and finally to a silence that affirms the unnerving silence of God. One simply endures what one cannot change, succumbing to self-isolation and a felt inability to communicate, resulting in a total silence that invites despair.

The way out of this dire predicament is modeled by the Psalmist in the sheer expression of emotion, of giving voice to oneself, breaking the silence. In the classic form of the lament, prayer becomes an act of subversion, and even of liberation. It is an active, as opposed to merely reactive, form of relation to God, a protest against an atheistic resignation to fate.[25] Gustavo Gutiérrez notes that the prayer of lament, in the form of Psalm 22, is uttered by Jesus himself on the cross: "My God, my God, why have you forsaken me?"

> All of these considerations do not eliminate the element of protest from the final words of Jesus; they are rather an attempt to situate it properly. Even in his lament Jesus 'spoke correctly of God.' His cry on the cross renders more audible and more penetrating the cries of all the Jobs, individual and collective of human history.[26]

For Sölle, this is what the Job story tells us: that far from a story of submission to what he cannot understand, the book is focused on Job's own self-expression before God. He draws God's attention because of his protest. He actively wrestles with his suffering, and with God's incomprehensibility. He does not simply submit to his suffering out of a sense of fate, much less accept the notion of a divinely ordained masochism. Especially in the face of his own just state, he recognizes that human rationales and theologies of suffering ultimately fail to justify it or even to exonerate God, for they cannot. The message of *Night* echoes here for Sölle: A God who causes suffering cannot be justified; a God who shares in our sufferings might be.

An active engagement with one's suffering, which perforce includes a protest against suffering, leads to a sense of solidarity with others who suffer and a desire to see their suffering end as well.[27] This solidarity emanates from a sorrow and even indignation over what meets our eyes, a sorrow that is in a certain sense the sorrow of God realized in and through the compassion of human beings. As Sölle puts it, this is "no alien sorrow" for "God has no other hands than ours" to be in solidarity with the living victims of history.[28]

This is where the cross really enters the picture for Sölle. God becomes a problem for people of faith when the cross is associated with a God who sends suffering to people, demanding the impossible.[29] This can imply a divine insensitivity to human misery, even a contempt for humanity.[30] The cross seems to be a reversal of the "humane progress" indicated in the divine reprieve in the story of Abraham's aborted sacrifice of his son Isaac.[31] But, perhaps worse, such a masochism, sanctioned by a view of a sadistic God, leads to patterns of submission[32] or mute endurance[33] in reaction to the sheer mute force of God. As we have seen in Simone Weil, the nature of affliction is that even as one feels accursed and absolutely distant from God, one is also situated at the foot of the cross of Christ.[34] In both cases, the cross is itself an expression of the blind mechanisms of fate, and chance, through which God works. "The blindness of the mechanism, its anonymity, the element of sheer chance, is at the heart of the experience of affliction."[35] But if we only see blind fate at work, are we not at risk of missing the essential revelation of God in the midst of affliction, an experience not unlike that of the distance between the Son and the Father, dramatically played out on Golgotha itself?

Sölle charts a Christian way out of such a conundrum. A proper understanding of the cross must be rooted, as we have noted, in a an expression of emotion, such as we find in the form of the laments in the Psalms. Even the utter despondency of Psalm 88 leads to a stance before God, something beyond mere submission or helpless reaction.[36] This then gives us the wherewithal to see our own

creaturely dignity before God, as did Job, ultimately uncomprehend-
ing as he was, and sets us on a course of liberation from suffering.
Johannes Metz points out that Rahner, too, says as much, when he
"very gently asks us to consider if there must not also be a place in
the church's proclamation and spirituality for complaint and for an
insistent questioning of God on the part of human beings faced with
the horrors of God's creation."[37]

Yet in the end, the cross is not the cross of Job, but the cross
of Jesus, the one who met it freely, with anguish, but without complaint. For Sölle the cross of Christ, then, is not a symbol of an
imposed masochism, nor even of silent endurance of what cannot
be changed, but rather a sign of the consequence of a love freely
undertaken, indeed freely suffered. The price of the avoidance of
suffering is ceasing to love; the cross is the sign that love has not
avoided suffering, but entered into suffering in solidarity with the
victims of suffering.[38] It is a realistic sign of things as they are, to
be sure, and that reality includes the places that love finally leads
us into, the forms that love finally assumes, in flesh and blood.
And it is in light of this reading of the cross that we find in Jesus'
own sufferings, including his utter aloneness and his waiting for the
scream to come forth,[39] an active acceptance born of a love that desires to share in the sufferings of others. Here we find his "heart of
assent."[40]

That heart of assent not only leads to the point of physical death,
but also leads Jesus *through* it. The very "repeatability" of Jesus' prayer
at Gethsemane ("not my will but yours be done")[41] includes the fact
that for the Christian, death is not the final word, but is a way through
to new life: "A Christian is a person for whom death is behind him."[42]
The revelation of the death and resurrection of Jesus is that God
loves us even when that love is not visible, but that love, joining
with the victims of suffering and history, makes a future possible.[43]
In theological terms, the cross must be seen as part of the Paschal
Mystery that extends from the incarnation to the triumph of hope
in the resurrection. It must be part of a revelation that points in and
through Jesus to the God whose love is so positive that it wants only
life and good — our life, our good.

But still, where God is to be found in relation to the sheer darkness of human suffering, so much of it hidden, remains a challenge.

The cross standing alone seems an insufficient theological response to the conundrums presented by suffering. Even if it does not invite one toward a posture of passive resignation, or a near morbid identification with the sufferings of Jesus, it does not intuitively or obviously stand as a symbol of hope. There is no question, of course, that Christian tradition poses that hope is in fact revealed in the cross. But we cannot arrive there simply by pointing to the cross and counseling those who suffer to offer up their sufferings or to join them to the sufferings of Jesus. Prima facie this makes little sense, and constitutes a rather shallow pastoral strategy. The cross must be seen, rather, in the context of the whole of the revelation of God in Jesus Christ, as a pivotal revelatory moment, but one that takes on its salvific meaning and aura of hope from its relation to both who Jesus was and how Jesus himself met with his own suffering. This is a topic that we take up again in chapter 5.

The Problem with Theodicy

We have noted already Sölle's reservations about theodicy, the philosophical attempt to justify God in the face of suffering, especially the suffering of innocents, and the reality of evil. Yet the dominant approach of the modern mind in the face of suffering has been not to look for the revelation of God in the cross of Jesus, but to put God under scrutiny. God must somehow be judged for either competence as a good and provident creator, one of the aims of theodicy, or for apparent maliciousness, and, perhaps worse, lack of concern about what God has created, the atheistic conclusion. This becomes an acute matter when the suffering of the innocent is taken into account. "Innocent" here could mean those "undeserving" of suffering (perhaps implying that some who suffer deserve it), or simply the suffering of those who happen to be in the wrong place at the wrong time, as in the so-called "collateral damage" of warfare, such as children and other non-combatants.

The origin of this modern fixation on God's relation to innocent suffering is actually quite ancient. In the Book of Job, it is the suffering of a just man and his family that puts God in the docket. The exchanges between Job and his "friends" circle not only around divine justice or lack of it shown toward Job, but whether God himself can be justified in the face of Job's sufferings. If God can be so justified, then the implication must be that Job is not in fact innocent. Underlying this argument, of course, is that God metes out suffering to us in accordance with our lack of virtue. Yet this line of argumentation doesn't compute for Job, who knows that he has been and remains essentially just. In the end, it is God himself, speaking from the whirlwind, who puts an end to this judicial and theological speculation: "Who is this that obscures divine plans with words of ignorance?" (Job 38:1)

Yet, the Book of Job is actually an exception to the biblical rule, for the massive weight of the biblical tradition has been to expect suffering as a part of human life, and that God does not wish to see his people suffer as they do. This leitmotif is established in Exodus, in the call of Moses, where God says:

> I have witnessed the affliction of my people in Egypt and have heard their cry of complaint against their slave drivers, so I know well what they are suffering. Therefore I have come down to rescue them from the hands of the Egyptians and lead them out of that land into a good and spacious land, a land flowing with milk and honey.... (Exod. 3:7–8)

This God who does not want to see his people suffer is the foundation of what will become the Mosaic Covenant. Biblical theology ultimately does not set out to justify God. In the face of innumerable ruptures with the Covenant, it is the people of God who must be justified, and whom God continually forgives. And, in the shadow of the cross, the burden is clearly shifted to human beings themselves, and to the dark history of sin that has resulted in so much suffering, suffering that is partly the work of human hands.

Despite this biblical tradition, placing God on the stand and trying to justify him before human suffering, particularly the suffering of the innocent, is very much the approach taken by modern philosophical and theological approaches to the problem of suffering. The problem of suffering has become a problem about God. This approach, called "theodicy" (from the Greek words for God [*theos*] and judgment [*dike*]) has tended to look at the problem of the "suffering of the innocent" as if the suffering of all of humanity, which is far from innocent, required no particular explanation beyond what could be explained by the justice of God's providence.[44]

The degree to which we should implicate God in the darkness of this world (or, for that matter, in its goodness) is the classic problem for theodicy, a probably succinctly expressed by John Hick: "If God is perfectly good, He must want to abolish all evil; if He is unlimitedly powerful, he must be able to abolish all evil: but evil exists; therefore either God is not perfectly good or He is not unlimitedly powerful."[45] The assumption here is that if we are to distinguish authentic Christian hope from facile optimism, or worse, from delusion, then the God in whom we hope had better be worth hoping in: a God perfectly good, unlimitedly powerful, and in no way the cause of suffering. Such a good God needs to be justified in the face of so much evidence to the contrary.

Many theologians today view such approaches toward justifying God through theodicy with increasing skepticism. American theologian John Thiel is one of many theologians in recent years who has undertaken a critical analysis of theodicy.[46] Beginning with Leibniz in the sixteenth century, he traces the development of the argument that God has created the best of all possible worlds, and that evil (and the suffering it generates) is the result of human freedom, a contingency which God has allowed for within a provident order of creation. God has created the best of all possible worlds, one that includes freedom, and his designs cannot be completely known. This "modern" view dovetails, in the end, with the "pre-modern" view, that no suffering is finally non-innocent; in some way human beings, by virtue of their freedom, are implicated in their own suffering. Such, according to Thiel, is part of the message of the Book of Job.

The "postmodern" view, by contrast, begins with the "best of all possible Gods" theories, exemplified by process theologies built out of the philosophical principles of Alfred North Whitehead and Charles Hartshorne, where God is ultimately inseparable from the inner movements of nature. In this approach, innocence is not an issue and God does not have to be justified before suffering per se. Rather, God works in and through suffering, which occurs as a by-product of natural processes, to bring about God's ends. But, according to Thiel, it is hard to get away from the conclusion here that God is himself complicit in suffering, not simply by allowing for it, but further, by being so deeply involved in the processes that bring it about.

A fourth and alternative view would be that God is a "witnessing presence" to a suffering that he does not wish to see. "A more effective approach to God's relation to evil would highlight God's presence and conceive of divine power as a graceful function of that presence."[47] Such a witnessing presence would serve to underscore the evil present in the suffering of the innocent, thus sparing those who suffer, or their suffering from being understood as a mere statistic or factum, a by-product of nature; and when suffering is the result of evil perpetrated by human moral agency, this witnessing presence of God would stand as a witness to "the scandal of victimization,"[48] the ultimate victim being Jesus Christ himself.[49] In both cases, "God neither permits, nor wills, nor causes any kind of suffering or death at all."[50] In the end, this might lead to a position not far from Schillebeeckx's view of God as pure positivity in the face of a suffering he does not in any way desire to see.[51]

Thiel concludes that the problem with theodicies is that they "deny the integrity of suffering either by attributing all suffering to human guilt as does the pre-modern view [traditional/classical approaches], or by transforming innocent suffering into a meaningful means of moral development, as does the modern view [Hick, Swinburne], or by removing innocent suffering from the scope of divine providence, as does the postmodern view."[52]

Fellow theologian Terrence Tilley takes issue with theodicies because they represent a calculus about suffering that fails to take into consideration the actual suffering of human beings. As such, theodicies devalue practical issues surrounding evil: they silence the cries of victims and marginalize their suffering; tend to valorize some forms of evil and minimize others; and ultimately promote complicity in injustice because systemic evils such as racism and sexism are rendered invisible.[53] Both Thiel and Tilley suggest that theories of God in relation to suffering that fail to take into account the sheer injustice of so much suffering, and that tend to distance God from those who suffer, are finally insupportable. Theologians Kenneth Surin and David Tracy concur, holding that the narratives of suffering people themselves must be taken into account. Tracy writes:

> To develop a theology today is to reject modern theodicies in their modern forms of purely theoretical solutions which, however finely tuned in argument and however analytically precise in concept, are somewhat beside the point — the point of facing with hope the horror while still speaking and acting at all by naming and thinking the God of genuine hope.

Referring to the plethora of theologies that have emerged since the Holocaust, along with the rise of voices of the oppressed and marginalized, he continues:

> All these new forms for theologies are grounded in a refusal to turn away from evil wherever and whenever it exists and a refusal to embrace any theodicy — indeed any theology — that ignores the suffering of any people or individual. Recall the haunting refrains of suffering and resistance, of strength, hope, and sometimes joy in the struggle in the songs and tales of oppressed peoples everywhere.[54]

I largely agree with this critique of theodicy, valuable as theodicies may be in gaining a philosophical distance from and objective stance toward the actual pain of human existence. Nevertheless, the underlying question of theodicy is an important one: Where does God stand in relation to all this real human suffering? How can we arrive at a theological understanding of suffering, one that puts God in such a relation to it that we find a path toward hope in the midst of life's real darkness?

A theological tradition running from Augustine through Aquinas would conclude that God, as the absolutely sovereign and free source of all that exists, is the one for whom all eventualities within freedom are given as possible and the one who can draw good out of all possibilities, even the bleakest, "if only we are willing."[55] This solution, however, does not make suffering comprehensible, either as consequence of sin or as divine judgment. It is still encountered as a surd, a stumbling block to comprehensive schemes of meaning.

While Christian faith cannot hold that a good and all-powerful God directly induces human suffering, it can hold that God is indirectly implicated in suffering which he does not cause, but mysteriously admits into the plan of divine providence. For example, Jacques Maritain, sounding somewhat like Leibniz, famously wrote:

> *Evil of nature*, or suffering, is the object neither of a *permission* nor of a *will properly so called* of God — let us say rather that it is *admitted* by God, in this sense that from the very fact that God wills and causes, as transcendent first Cause, the good of the material universe and of the things of this universe, He causes at the same stroke, but *indirectly* and *per accidens* or in an *extraintentional* manner, the losses and evils linked inevitably and by nature to the goods and to the gains in question (no generation without corruption, no life without some destruction, nor any passage to a superior form of life without some death)....[56]

Maritain carves out a position here somewhat different from the classical (pre-modern) approach of Augustine and Aquinas, where God permits evil because God has created all things in freedom. Here, the issue is not evil by permission, which could imply some level of intentionality, but evil as an indirect consequence of the created order which God has providentially ordained toward an ultimate good. This is not the Whiteheadian god of process, to be sure; God is decidedly distinct from creation. But, perhaps not unlike Leibniz, Maritain seems to be concluding here that what we have is the best of all possible worlds, one rendered so by divine providence.

Mystery of Suffering, Mystery of God

In contrast to this approach, we can turn to the work of Karl Rahner, which he treated in his classic essay, "Why Does God Allow Us to Suffer?"[57] In this essay, Rahner held that the attempt to answer why God allows us to suffer can tell us something important about God. But to ask the question "Why does God allow us to suffer?" possibly looks for an answer found partly outside God himself, in a moral or metaphysical calculus, a theodicy. While Rahner did not reject the classical distinction between God's causing evil or simply permitting it, nor even the legitimacy of theodicy itself, he claimed that these classical approaches do not finally explain *why* God allows suffering, but only how it can be said *that* God allows it. Agreeing to an extent with the classical approach, Rahner held that all we can say with certainty is that God has created all things in freedom to allow for their optimal good, as well as the good of the whole of creation, and that in that freedom God allows the darkness of evil, of which suffering and death are the primary exemplars. Beyond this, we finally have to admit that the question itself is unanswerable, that we are in a region of incomprehensibility, because suffering itself is ultimately incomprehensible.

But, more emphatically than the classical tradition did, Rahner wanted to preserve the sense of God's holy mystery, encountered here as God's ultimate incomprehensibility. Thus, he would move beyond the classical distinctions, such as we see in Maritain. "Having regard to God's omnipotent freedom, which knows no bounds, causing and permitting seem to us to come so closely together that we can ask quite simply why God allows us to suffer, without having to distinguish *a priori* in this divine 'allowing' [*Lassen*] between God's permitting [*Zulassen*] and causing [*Bewirken*]."[58] And so he preferred to say that God "allows" [*läßt*] suffering. In the case of the sufferings brought on by nature (e.g., earthquakes) or involving the processes of nature (e.g., disease), Rahner admitted the validity of the distinction between God's "permitting" suffering and God's "causing" suffering, but he opted for saying that God "allows" such suffering, because the term "allow...does not make the traditional distinctions, for instance, between permitting and causing" which have led to metaphysical impasses.[59]

To press this further, let us focus for a moment on the suffering attending disease. The suffering generated by some diseases is entangled in the ambiguity of our moral state. Some diseases, notably AIDS, but also various venereal diseases, some forms of hepatitis, and sometimes even lung cancer, reflect this ambiguity in that they involve both the physical and moral domains: they are often clinical states of disease usually brought on in part as a result of acts involving the exercise of some degree of human freedom, although the degree of freedom varies widely from one person to another. Still, the claim is often made that because human freedom is involved at all, the physical and spiritual suffering brought on by some diseases such as AIDS is "self-earned" and, further, even ordained by God as a kind of judgment for sin. Following this line of argumentation, we are no longer speaking of innocent suffering as a result of accidents of the created order somehow providentially "admitted" by God into the created order.

Rahner, on the other hand, refrained from entering into such judgments, resting content with the more enigmatic formulation that God *allows* such suffering.[60] In order to maintain a sense of God as mystery, Rahner maintained God's absolute sovereignty in freedom and power, so that we reach a point at which it is impossible for the finite mind to sustain the classical distinctions between what God ordains by "permission" within the ambit of human freedom, and what God "permits" or "admits" through indirect causality. The difficulty with the classical distinction becomes evident when trying to find the meaning in a disease like AIDS that involves the sufferings brought on both by the perplexity of human existence and by the physical vicissitudes of a clinical condition that follows its own natural course. In this case, neither of the classical positions, divine permission of evil within a schema of freedom, or indirect causality of it by God's providentially admitting it into creation, is adequate. And, to go further and say that God permits the suffering of disease in order, for example, to draw the sufferer closer to God, or in order to make people more moral, is to risk making claims about the divine prerogatives that lie beyond human competency; and it implies some divine will or intentionality, at least in the minimalist form of a permission of suffering. To propose that God indirectly causes the suffering of disease could lead to the conclusion that the disease is some kind of divine judgment. Both classical views search for a moral or metaphysical calculus that would elevate disease to a metaphysical state, as well as describe and even limit the freedom and omnipotence of God, resulting in a diminishment of God's mystery.

Of course, the conditions for the possibility of sin are given with the divine gift of freedom, and sin is often intertwined with physical suffering. According to Rahner, "sin arising from creaturely freedom (which is never absolute) is itself by its very nature interwoven in an indissoluble and undelimitable way with other suffering. . . . "[61] Yet it is theologically perilous to say that moral evil, much less the physical consequences so intimately connected with human sinfulness, can be said to be caused by God, even indirectly. While we can understand sin to be the ontological foundation or ground of suffering, as Augustine, following Paul, did in his understanding of original sin, we certainly cannot say that sin is caused by God, even indirectly, any more than God could have caused, even indirectly, the sinfulness that led to the suffering of the crucifixion. This would amount to a set-up by God of the suffering of Jesus on the cross. Nor, for Rahner, can the physical consequences of the moral perplexity that eventuates in sin be said to be caused by God, but again, only *allowed* by God.

Rahner avoided the language of causality (sin leads to suffering, or, by implication, suffering is the consequence of sin and the experience of divine judgment) in order to stress that God is responsible for the whole of creation in freedom, a claim which includes not only the possibility of evil and suffering, apparent and real, natural and moral, but *also* the possibility of grace given and received in the heart of sin and suffering. In other words, Rahner finally avoided classical theodicy in order to leave room for hope in a God who, mysteriously, can be encountered in the heart of suffering itself, which is itself finally incomprehensible.[62] God does not stand outside of suffering, but is found within it. Suffering simply cannot be mapped out according to schemes that would pit divine justice against human sinfulness, or that would place God outside the world of suffering itself.

Raising the question, then, "Why does God allow us to suffer?" probes into the reality of God, who is incomprehensible mystery, one whose transcendence is found in the depths of human experience, including the mystery of suffering. Rahner thus famously concluded: "The incomprehensibility of suffering is part of the incomprehensibility of God."[63] The incomprehensibility of suffering, in turn, is a "limit" experience that takes us to the edge of the incomprehensible, that is, God. This is not to say that we have here the reason for suffering, as if suffering were intelligible; this is simply to express where suffering leads us, to the incomprehensible mystery of God. God is the blinding light revealed in the darkness of suffering. As Job finally sees: "I know that you can do all things, and that no purpose of yours can be thwarted.... There I have uttered what I did not understand, things too wonderful for me, which I did not know" (Job 42:2–3).

In the failure of a moral or metaphysical calculus to explain it, suffering can lead to despair, and ultimately, in death, to perdition; but seen as a liminal experience that leads us to the edge of the divine incomprehensibility, it can also be the "beginning of redeemed finality in God."[64] That is to say, it can be a pathway of hope leading to final joy.

In the end, the question of why God allows suffering leads to our surrendering to the sacred — to the One who is, in the last analysis, sovereign in freedom and love, and who in that freedom and love submitted to suffering and death, to be revealed as the God who is intimately present within every moment of human existence, even within suffering. But any of this can be said only in light of the cross, which is the sign that God has entered into and gone through all — and in the victory of life over death, is "all in all" (1 Cor. 15:28).

In this way, we retrieve the cross as a symbol of hope, not only for the innocent victims of history, but for all who live out histories of suffering. All are in need of a hope grounded in the real and not in denial of life as it is. All are in need of a hope that acknowledges human fears in the face of the suffering entailed on life's road, a hope that leads us through suffering to new configurations of life.

Chapter Four

The Cross as Locus
of the Divine Empathy

"Where can we go? Escape — escape from God? But how, my poor, unhappy Brother Leo, how?"

"We can take another road, Brother Francis."

"There will be lepers on every road we take. You'll see, the streets will become filled with them. They will not disappear until we have fallen into their arms. So, Brother Leo, put on a bold front — we're going forward."[1]
— Nikos Kazantzakis

IN THE NOVEL *Saint Francis* by Nikos Kazantzakis, the Saint prays to God to ask what more God might be asking of him. He has already restored the Church of San Damiano and given up everything else for God. Yet he is riddled with fear of contact with lepers. He confides to Brother Leo: "Even when I'm far away from them, just hearing the bells they wear to warn passers-by to keep their distance is enough to make me faint." God's response to Francis's prayer is precisely what he does not want to hear: he must face his fears and embrace the next leper he sees on the road. Soon he hears the dreaded clank of the leper's bell. Yet, Francis moves through his fears, embraces the leper, and even kisses his wounds. Jerome Miller describes the importance of this scene:

> Only when he embraced that leper, only when he kissed the very ulcers and stumps he had always found abhorrent, did he experience for the first time that joy which does not come from this world and which he would later identify with the joy of

crucifixion itself. . . . If Francis felt drawn to the leper instead of compelled to recoil from him, it was because he saw embedded in the wounds of this outcast the priceless gem of his own nothingness. The joy which has often been recognized as characteristic of the saints . . . springs right from that wound as from its original source . . . What we avoid when we turn away from [the outcasts] is the original wound we have buried as deeply as we can inside ourselves. The joy of the saints comes from reopening it.[2]

As this selection from Jerome Miller's book reminds us, it is only by driving into the reality of suffering, and not evading it, that one can find a pathway to hope and encounter with the sacred. This insistence on penetrating the reality of suffering leads us to consider what kind of theological formulation might capture this stance. For we want to do so in such a way that the path of the cross is also a path to a hope rooted in realism. It is here that we turn to Rahner's later writings, and particularly what he calls "Christian pessimism." Our focus here is not only on penetrating the reality of *my* suffering, but the dark suffering of others, of "the outcasts" or those we would rather put beyond the scope of our awareness because their suffering is too horrible and frightening to draw near. For dark suffering is the suffering of the world in which I participate; it is the history of bodily, psychic, and spiritual pain that has afflicted great numbers of people, but which also attends my own situation as a human being. We shall see that this path leads to a view of the cross where empathy, the divine empathy, pours forth like balm onto the wounds of lepers.

AIDS as Metaphor

The AIDS epidemic, a major source of suffering and death on a universal scale and respecting of no human distinctions, is representative of dark suffering, suffering as it is encountered on broad historical and social scales, but also in the irreducible uniqueness of individual human lives. Despite some gains in halting the rate of the spread of this disease, the statistics on its advance continue to lead to discouragingly dire, even apocalyptic, conclusions about the fate of very many people on the planet, and especially the most poor and vulnerable. The sheer force of this disease and its impact on the lives of millions and millions of people hardly need to be established today.

Further, AIDS has a kind of metaphorical quality. It is unique as a relatively new disease, but as a form of human suffering it can shed new light on approaches to other forms of manifold suffering. Echoing Sontag on this point, an MIT-sponsored study of AIDS states:

> All illnesses are metaphors. They absorb and radiate the personalities and social conditions of those who experience symptoms and treatments. Only a few illnesses, however, carry such cultural salience that they become icons of the times. Like tuberculosis in *fin de siècle* Europe, like cancer in the first half of the American century, and like leprosy from Leviticus to the present, AIDS speaks of the menace and losses of the times. It marks the sick person, encasing the afflicted in an exoskeleton of peculiarly powerful meanings: the terror of a lingering and untimely death, the panic of contagion, the guilt of "self-earned illness."[3]

Given this metaphorical quality of AIDS, many of the questions AIDS raises have broad reach beyond the disease itself, and may extend to other forms of suffering that not only afflict individual persons but implicate entire communities and societies.

Furthermore, AIDS continues to rivet the religious imagination. Among the reasons for this is surely the fact that there come together in AIDS a number of factors that cannot be escaped: a congruence of changing patterns of sexuality (both homosexual and heterosexual); of religiously and socially proscribed behaviors or practices such as intravenous drug usage; and of suffering and terminal disease on a massive scale, especially among the legions of hidden poor. When AIDS arrived with a deceptively quiet force upon the world around 1981, it was immediately clear that this disease would pose a challenge to some established paradigms in Catholic theology, at least in moral theology, by virtue of its very newness and complexity.[4] More than other diseases, AIDS in particular links sexuality, appetite, disease, guilt, shame, suffering, and death in ways that only grow more complex when we factor them into the manifolds of poverty, race, gender, class, culture, and religion — all projected now onto a global map. Like death itself, AIDS demands not only a pastoral response, but theological attention, in order to plumb the reality of suffering it presents for any intelligibility within the context of faith.

Indeed, we are compelled to approach AIDS within the theological terrain of faith, rather than relegate it to the realm of spirituality or pastoral practice alone, as if AIDS had nothing substantial to contribute to the understanding of faith in Christ. A professed compassion for its suffering victims that does not issue from and lead to a deeper penetration of its reality would constitute a deficient form of lived faith. The empathy of Jesus, which led to his own entrance into the worlds of those outcasts for whom he showed compassion, even to the point of joining them on their crosses, was a pathway to God, as Francis came to know firsthand.

It seems obvious even to the casual observer that, as with all calamitous evils, AIDS puts God into question. More precisely, it asks: What does it mean to hope in God in the midst of seeming hopelessness, without denying the utter darkness of the sorrow of AIDS? And further, how can an answer to this theological question ground a compassionate pastoral response, a solidarity with the afflicted that issues *from* Christian faith and does not simply stand alongside it?

Rahner's Christian Pessimism

Karl Rahner's theology of "Christian pessimism" offers a theological framework within which the experience of AIDS and, by extension, other forms of suffering, can be interpreted and its suffering pastorally embraced. As I stated in the Preface, the starting point for Rahner's theology is an unflinching acceptance of the full reality of the human condition, a commitment to truth — to begin with what is the case. In this aspect, we find striking parallels between Rahner's approach to the real and that of William Lynch and Jerome Miller.[5] But Rahner is also part of a great pantheon of twentieth-century theologians who gazed upon the human condition and concluded that Christianity could allow no escape from the real and that it is a command of Christian life to enter fully into it. This is the demand of the cross. And if the demand of the cross can only be found by facing and penetrating the reality of suffering which marks the "real" in a Christian theological sense, this is because the real is made sacred by virtue of the incarnation, the entry of God into human flesh and blood.

Among twentieth-century theologians before Rahner, Reinhold Niebuhr especially brought home the importance of the real in his writings on the nature and destiny of the human race in the face of the historical evidences of sin. Like Karl Barth before him, Niebuhr arrived at a realistic and historically pessimistic view of the human race and its sheerly historical destiny.

> The qualified optimism of an adequate religion will never satisfy the immature minds who have found some superficial harmony in the world in which the evils and threats to meaning are not taken into account. Nor will it satisfy those who think that every ill from which man suffers can be eliminated in some proximate future. It will nerve men to exhaust all their resources in building a better world, in overcoming human strife, in mitigating the fury of man's injustice to man, and in establishing a society in which some minimal security for all can be achieved.

Still, there is room for hope:

> ... [I]n an adequate religion there will be a recognition of the fact that nothing accomplished along the horizontal line of history can eliminate the depth of life which is revealed at every point of history.[6]

Beset by sin, humanity is in need of a redemption that will be its source of final hope. That redemption is accomplished by the cross, a symbol of the entry into the bloody history of the human race of the saving God of Israel. There is no authentic Christianity apart from the cross.[7]

Still, if the cross is to stand as a symbol of hope, there is some need to explain the unusual expression, "Christian pessimism," which sets the context for what follows. In light of this notion of Christian pessimism, I will raise again the question of the relation of God to the sufferer, and ask how the notion of divine empathy revealed in the cross can serve as a foundation for hope.

It would be a serious mistake to presume that "Christian pessimism" is a counsel toward morbidity. Rahner's own delight in the joys of life is well attested and was expressed as a lyrical motif in many of his writings. Rahner was first of all a Christian, one who believed that where sin abounds, there grace abounds yet more (Rom. 5:21). In Rahner's own words, "...Christianity is a message of joy, courage, and unshakable confidence."[8] But Rahner was also a sober realist. He had lived through much personal and family darkness, about which he was mostly reticent. He also lived in the shadows of two world wars, in both of which his native Germany was defeated, and in the second of which he lost not only his dear friend, Alfred Delp, but witnessed the bombing and destruction of his homeland and the reduction of much of Europe to rubble.

Many of us remember those long nights in an air-raid shelter during the war, when we stood in abysmal loneliness among a crowd of terror-stricken people, waiting for death. In the darkness, we felt the coldness of fear chilling our hearts, and it was in vain that we put up a show of courage and stiff upper lip: our brave words were hollow, and fell as husks about our feet, leaving only silence and the explosion came, and the shower of debris to bury us. Let this be taken as the symbol of modern life. We have indeed crawled out from the powdered shelters; we have resumed our daily lives with a great show of bravery and pretence of enjoyment; but the truth is that many of us are as though we had remained buried in the debris, because we have suffered no change of heart through having been brushed by the wing of death. However far fetched it may sound, it remains true that externals are but the shadow of what has taken place in the depths of our hearts. Our hearts are obstructed, buried under debris.[9]

Rahner was no stranger to suffering on both deeply personal and broad historical scales, nor to the lessons it would force upon us.

In a short address entitled "Christian Pessimism," published near the end of his career, Rahner described our human predicament as one of "radical perplexity."[10] Taking his cue from 2 Corinthians 4:8– 10, "we are perplexed, but not driven to despair," Rahner argued that perplexity is a permanent existential, a given fact of human life, an integral dimension of human existence. It does not force us to despair, but as a permanent existential it will not be overcome within the span of human life itself. It will only be overcome within the ambit of God's provident mercy, the fulfillment of which takes place in God's future, which Christian theology calls the eschaton.

In some of his later writings, Rahner elaborated upon this radical perplexity. He meant, first, that life is ultimately uncontrollable by human means, by Promethean thrusts toward knowledge and manipulation of reality undertaken on our own. As Lynch established so persuasively in *Images of Hope,* we cannot heal ourselves; we need help to imagine or envision new scenarios for life. For in the midst of our perplexity, human life becomes a dauntingly uncontrollable reality; no one theory about its meaning, no politics or technology, no genetics or medical technique, no psychology or therapy, not even one philosophy or theology, can encompass the entire mystery of human existence, much less "fix" it.

Second, Christian hope in an unrealized future can include the conviction that things "here below" will only get worse before they get better. Just as human beings cannot redeem themselves, human history cannot be redeemed by human beings. This idea is developed in some of Rahner's later essays. In one of his darkest writings, he muses:

> Although we may still hear the echoes of a triumphant humanism that claims to have reached the limits of its self-made fulfillment, today we are assailed by a feeling that we have lost our way, a feeling that all our beautiful ideals are quickly becoming threadbare. Dissonant voices urge us to do a thousand things at once; hopelessness is spreading so inexorably that all

ideals, old and new, all programs for the future, which still have a following, look pitiful and lack impact.[11]

What Heidegger termed "calculative thinking"[12] has proved to be a path toward dead ends because it cannot begin to encompass this perplexity. We have finally begun to doubt the limits of science itself. In the face of this perplexity, faith truly must lie in what we hope for but do not yet see (Heb. 11:1). Our salvation does not lie within history itself.

Evil continues to insinuate itself into the heart of this radically finite reality, mutating into ever new forms, sinister and devastating, often bringing about intense suffering and even the destruction of very good lives. This aspect of perplexity pertains to the darkness of human existence, our entanglements in sin, suffering, and death that come to light in tragedy and tragic reversal, as we saw in the work of Jerome Miller. There is also the darkness of anguish, of confronting the truth about ourselves, of coming up against the imprisonments of our lives, and facing full throttle the complexities of our moral, physical, and spiritual selves in relation to others and to God. The experience of facing truth can be accompanied by the sickness of confusion because what one sees is how perplexing life is, an admixture of great goodness of desire and incalculable failure and loss, mixed, as Simone Weil saw it, with a dose of unforgiving fate.

But the darkness of human existence that we are concerned with here involves more than one's own tragic reversals, cosmic in their implications as they may be. Darkness here includes the mass of suffering that takes place on a wide, even universal scale. AIDS, for example, is a form of suffering that has produced waves of physical, emotional, and spiritual suffering throughout whole continents. The person who receives an AIDS diagnosis knows full well the meaning of darkness in both its personal and wider historical dimensions, for she, an irreducibly unique human person, faces a terrifying tragic reversal in her own life, and she is also participating in a global catastrophe, often enough entrapped by the circumstances of her life and her illness. The survivors of the genocide in Rwanda and Sudan have had a similar experience: profound suffering on a personal level that is constituted in its very nature by being part of an incomprehensibly larger theater of agony. This darkness, in both its global and personal aspects, is part of the human condition in general; as a part of human reality, we ignore it at our own peril.

The Christian, therefore, is entitled, even called, to be a realist, indeed, a kind of "pessimistic" realist, because faith " ... obliges [us] to see this existence as dark and bitter and hard, and as an unfathomable and radical risk."[13] There are no short-range answers to this harsh aspect of reality on the human side of the scale. Only by running the risk of this existence and embracing the sorrows that it brings in its wake, as did God in Jesus, can one begin to speak of hope.

Christian pessimism, then, describes the experience of being a Christian within the perplexing and often dark reality of existence. But this is not an everyday sort of pessimism, a despondency bordering on despair, or a thinly veiled cynicism, much less a suppressed rage. No, this pessimism is a "Christian" pessimism because it is precisely in the experience of perplexity that Jesus knew in Gethsemane and on the Cross that the Christian finds hope, not as the possibility of an escape from suffering, but as the locus of the encounter with God. It is within reality that Christian faith believes God to have been most fully revealed in relation to us.

Rahner thus held two terms together in an uneasy unity in this expression: the "pessimism" deriving from an unflinching realism before the human condition, and the "Christian" hope for human beings that can only begin within what is excruciatingly real. But we must always keep in mind that reality for the Christian also includes that which cannot be seen ("seen and unseen" says the Nicene Creed), that which is promised as our hope. So in facing the crosses of existence, and in going through their sufferings, we do so in anticipation of a fulfillment of human existence that is promised by God but not yet fully seen. One is reminded again of Reinhold Niebuhr: "The mystery of life is comprehended in meaning, though no human statement of the meaning can fully resolve the mystery. The tragedy of life is recognized, but faith prevents tragedy from being pure tragedy. Perplexity remains, but there is no perplexity unto despair. Evil is neither accepted as inevitable nor regarded as a proof of the meaninglessness of life."[14]

With this preliminary sketch in mind, we can now focus briefly on three dimensions of Christian pessimism: its radical realism about life's imprisonments, its recognition that suffering is partly rooted in the reality of sin, and its embrace of the moral ambiguity of the human condition. As will become apparent in the paragraphs that follow, these three characteristics of Christian pessimism can be separated out from one another only with considerable artifice: Christian pessimism is a constellation of a robust realism, a sense of entanglement in sin, and a surrender to life's uncertainties.

Realism

In his *Foundations of Christian Faith,* Rahner writes that the Christian is "a person who accepts without reservations the whole of concrete human life with all of its adventures, its absurdities, and its incomprehensibilities." The Christian is called upon to accept reality as it is rather than to evade it through a false religious piety. One must face squarely and with appropriate humiliation the stark reality of sin — one's own, and the world's — and ultimately of the suffering and death that are, at least indirectly, the tragic consequences of sin. Human freedom is made actual in the context of a profound acceptance of self and of reality, "without leaving anything out, and without closing [oneself] to the totality of what in the ultimate depths of reality is inescapably imposed upon [humankind] as a task."[15]

In adopting this realism, we find that there is much that people cannot find a way to change, and this fact seriously shapes their future. Rahner used the dramatic metaphor of "imprisonment" to describe much of human existence, to denote that which is finally inescapable (somewhat akin to Weil's notion of force or Lynch's notion of entrapment), and also, more neutrally, to denote the sheer force of the objective reality that we are born into and through which in fact we exercise our freedom and actualize ourselves as persons: our gender, constitution, orientations, cultures, intelligence, imagination, and the like. None of these factors absolutely determines my freedom, but none is completely under my final control, either. We are bound within a radical finitude that resolves finally in death. But hope for a final freedom from suffering is found by living within the imprisonments of this finitude and also by living through them. A "... Christian believes that there is a path to freedom which lies in going through this imprisonment." This freedom is not simply gained by endurance, or sheer will power in overcoming obstacles. Rahner insisted, "We do not seize it by force, but rather it is given to us by God insofar as he gives himself to us through all of the imprison-ments of our existence."[16] As we accept God's self-gift, this gift of freedom, we are empowered to go through reality as it is, even within the confines of our various imprisonments. We saw a similar insight clearly at work in the thought of both Lynch and Miller in the last chapter. What Rahner adds is that our "going through" is not a sheer act of will; it is the grace-assisted actualization of our freedom.

Sin

"To be imprisoned" is to be subject to the sin of the world. In Rahner's theology, "original sin" implies an objective history of entanglements in guilt, and this history helps shape human freedom, both individual and interpersonal.[17] This entanglement in guilt is, as it were, thus "passed on" from one generation to the next as a permanent mark of the human condition within history. It is ratified within the multitude of personal histories of sin. All people thus participate in the sin of the world, a sin that exists, seemingly, from the beginning (*ab origine*) of the human race and its history.

This notion of the sin of the world leans on what Rahner means by freedom. Christians can understand themselves to be free persons in the sense that the human person is constituted as transcendental "openness to ... everything without exception ... truth, love, beauty, goodness, the absolute."[18] This freedom is played out within the concrete, real dimensions of existence when people enter into re-lationship with other human beings and thus realize their identity as unique spiritual persons, precisely in relation to others. Succes-sive acts of freedom help determine the final state of our lives, for which each person is finally responsible, a responsibility held within the ambit and embrace of God's mercy. Yet we cannot actualize this freedom in an absolutely unhindered way, as though we were monads in self-possession of utterly pure, abstracted natures. The actualization of our freedom takes place within a set of historical determining factors and in mutual relationship with other persons and their limitations. Rahner says that we "co-determine" one another, not only promoting our mutual freedom, but also through the limitations on our freedom that accrue from the history of sin. The actualization of human freedom is thus co-determined by what Rahner terms the "guilt" of the world, the actual burden of sin — a mutually shared history of guilt.[19]

Families illustrate well this co-determination by guilt. A family tree can be as much a picture of entanglement in guilt as it is a diagram of life. As we develop a unique identity within a family, we gradually differentiate ourselves from the others and discover our own personality and vocation. But this discovery is not simply the result of an autonomous act of self-development. We are shaped by our home environment, including its moral deficits, as well as by our peers, churches, schools, media, and numerous other factors. We do not emerge as the unique persons that we are in abstraction from the concrete historical conditions and the ideals and histories of the other people with whom we must interact, nor in abstraction from their guilt. Our lives "bear the stamp" of the history of other persons.[20] Any consideration of the human predicament has to take into account the reality of sin and the incongruous ratifications of it in our conditioned freedom, shaped as it is by the conditioned freedom of others.

Ambiguity

The reality of sin makes our lives morally ambiguous. As Rahner states: "[E]ven a person's most ideal, most moral act of freedom enters tragically into the concrete in an appearance which, because co-determined by guilt, is also the appearance of its opposite."[21] Just as grace meets and transfigures the darkness of life, making room for patterns of goodness, so, too, does guilt in many subtle ways affect the good acts of a good person.

... [T]he good act itself always remains ambiguous because of the co-determination of this situation by guilt. It always remains burdened with consequences which could not really be intended because they lead to tragic impasses, and which disguise the good that was intended by one's own freedom.[22]

What I may intend as a gesture of love may turn out to be an act of selfish domination, one "lured on" by cupidity, to borrow a phrase from Bernard of Clairvaux.[23] Conversely, even the experience of grace is not without ambiguity within the contours of what Paul terms the flesh.

This means that free decisions are not always undertaken without complication, even pain. Thus, truly free decisions are painful: "All of [human] experience points in the direction that there are in fact objectifications of personal guilt in the world which, as the material for the free decisions of other persons, threaten these decisions, have a seductive effect upon them, and make free decisions painful."[24] But, under most normal circumstances, painful though they may be, they are not absolutely impossible. There is a path to freedom even in the conditioned and perplexing state within which that exercise takes place. The actualization of freedom can result in either an objectification of grace or an objectification of guilt, or, more usually, some admixture of both.

Christian pessimism, thus understood, offers a theological context for facing suffering of the magnitude of AIDS: it is utterly realistic about the darkness of life's imprisonments; it presumes our entanglement in the sin of the world and our mystifying ratifications of it; and it acknowledges the moral and existential ambiguity of the human condition, the admixture of guilt and grace, within which AIDS, as a form of dark suffering, is generated. But it is also a theology of hope, a hope discovered, as Francis did, by entering into the reality of the leper. If what we seek is an account of our hope, then we need to go down that road and inquire more deeply into the suffering and death that AIDS brings in its wake. How, standing soberly within and participating in the suffering of global catastrophes of life, such as AIDS, can a Christian face suffering and death and still lay claim to hope?

Disclosure of the Divine Empathy

As we have already noted, Christian pessimism is above all a theology of hope in *God's* final victory over suffering and death, not a victory of our own making. Still, rather than run the risk of an overly optimistic view of God, the God who allows suffering and death, who draws good from all things, and who is ultimately victorious in what we call resurrection, we instead must ask: Is God somehow to be found within suffering and death, and not just a transcendent observer of it? Is God's empathy merely a formal statement about God, or does God somehow show the divine empathy by participating in our sufferings? And how might answers to these questions inform our approach to the human suffering engendered by AIDS?

Unlike Sobrino, Moltmann, and others, Rahner did not endorse the notion of a suffering or crucified God. He found this formulation unacceptable on the grounds that to posit a God who actually suffers is to posit a God who is so mired in the contingent and the finite, so miserable, that the transcendent glory in which we hope could seem to be purely mythical. The notion of hope thus becomes a mere theological construction. Nor in any way did Rahner wish to eclipse, with a theology of divine suffering, the actual, real suffering that human beings alone endure. Metz himself put it well:

> Rahner's hesitation, indeed, his refusal, to talk of a suffering God has something to do with his fundamental theological re-spect for the suffering and history of suffering of humanity. ...He also resists any attempt to get around human suffering by grasping it as God's suffering and sharing of suffering. De-spite the highly respectable attempts in contemporary Catholic as well as Protestant theology... nowhere has he joined in this discourse about the suffering God, about suffering between God and God [sic], about suffering in God. ... He insisted on respect for the nontransferable negative mystery of human suffering, which humankind may not begrudge God, for the sake of God and for the sake of humankind. "To put it very primitively — it does not help me at all to get out of my dirty mess and my despair just because things are going just as badly for God."[25]

Then does God stand aloof? Is there any divine involvement? Is hope in fact an illusion, the expression of a religious myth? Here for Rahner is where the full humanity of Jesus becomes crucial, for the Word of God made flesh "must be God's own reality," even as it remains a free human reality.[26] On the cross Jesus surrenders himself in death to the incomprehensible God. Because he is "God's own reality" made flesh, it can be said that God is intimately present in that surrender, for God is in real relation to Jesus through the incarnation. In a formally real way, then, God participates in the suffering and death of Jesus, who is nevertheless a free human being. And so, too, by analogy from the self-giving of God in the incarnation to the self-communication of God in grace, even grace darkly given, it can be said that God somehow enters into our suffering and death, or is communicating God's self to human beings even as they suffer.

But how? One approach might be that God is present to human suffering in a mode of empathic love, much as a mother is present within the suffering of her child through empathy, in what Michael Dodds has called an "empathic union." Like Rahner, Dodds bases his argument on the theologically legitimate predicate nominative, "Jesus is God." This means that Jesus' suffering is in some sense God's own. Dodds illustrates this empathic union with the love of a mother for her suffering child:

> The mother may be hardly at all aware of her own feeling of sadness, being conscious only of her child's pain, which she somehow experiences as her own. Here the lack of any reaction of sadness or suffering in her, distinct from the suffering of her child, points not to apathy, but to the profundity of her love.[27]

So, in a true sense, Jesus can be said to be the empathy of God. If this is the case, then in some real sense, God can be said to be empathic, just as a mother is in relation to her suffering child. And, with the same Christological understanding, one could go a step further and even speak of the "sorrow of God," a sorrow expressed by God through the freely bestowed compassion of Jesus for the sick, the suffering, the grieving, and even the dead, as in the case of his friend Lazarus.[28] Thus, in Jesus, the sorrows of the human lot are really met by the sorrow of God in and through the one who wept over the fate of Jerusalem, who bore our griefs, and who was despised and rejected by many: the man of sorrows.

The Dominican preacher Gerald Vann foreshadowed this approach while writing against the backdrop of the horrors of the Second World War. How, people wondered, can so much suffering, or any suffering, happen under the gaze of a loving God? Did God suffer along with God's people? Vann said that, in a sense, we can say, "God suffered" without compromise to the divine transcendence. Vann then explained what he meant:

> When I share in the suffering of someone I love, that actual sharing is the expression of something deeper, something permanent: the will-to-share, which is what we call love. And so in the mystery of redemption: the actual sharing is done through the humanity of Christ, but that actual sharing is the expression of deeper and permanent mystery in the Godhead, the will-to-share, i.e., the will to be a *companion*.[29]

Here we can find what is later developed as solidarity in the writings of theologians such as Sölle and Sobrino, while avoiding the suggestion of a suffering within the divine godhead, the Trinity itself, as suggested by Moltmann.

This divine empathy is shown most definitively on the cross. God sees fit that the suffering and dying of Jesus, which mark his entire life, become the revelation of the divine empathy, and ultimately, of God's response to the perplexity of existence.[30] The cross is thus indispensable for a Christian confrontation of the sorrow of AIDS and its harvest of death. Darkness yields to hope because the sorrow of those who suffer this disaster is met by the empathy of God. The Church can counsel compassion not alongside its theology, but in concert with it, because the empathy of God is itself revealed in the cross of Christ. It is this divine will to share, to be a companion in suffering and dying, revealed in the empathy manifested in the incarnate and crucified one, which finally grounds the Church's call to compassion for people with AIDS, or its response to any human being caught up in catastrophic suffering.

Yet this divine empathy is not always obvious, as those who suffer themselves well know. As St. Ignatius of Loyola saw when he advised in the Third Week of his Spiritual Exercises to consider how the divinity hides itself in the cruelty of the sufferings of Jesus on the cross, the cross thus introduces a wholly new and radically real horizon into the view of human consciousness. Rather than standing only as an obvious symbol of divine suffering, a point well made by such theologians as Moltmann, Sobrino, and others, it also stands as a statement that God is actually encountered, in hidden ways, in the sufferings of human life. The danger in overlooking the cross and what it stands for lies in the possible eclipse of a transcendent horizon which, were it recognized, could alter the personal as well as social and cultural patterns that govern much of life.

Christian pessimism describes a faith stance planted firmly in the dark reality of human existence. It is properly *pessimistic* because, from the standpoint of human experience, it boldly admits the reality, sinfulness, and ambiguity of life found in the entanglements of sin, suffering, and death that come to light in tragedy, and claims that there are no short-range answers to this dark reality on the human side of the scale. At the same time, it is properly a *Christian* pessimism because it is precisely in the experience of darkness that the Christian finds hope, not as the possibility of an exit from suffering, but as the possibility of something better, brought about not simply by oneself, but (*pace* Lynch) with help from beyond oneself. This hope for something better brought about by divine empathy is revealed in the cross. The brutal reality of the cross, entered into and not shunned, even by God, is paradoxically the root of our hope.

The Christian is a person who can say that God is for us, for me, and for our salvation precisely within this brutal reality, because God has been revealed in Jesus as the God of empathy. While the Christian cannot see the final outcome of human existence, hope is firm because God's empathy is really shown amidst the most brutal suffering. This hope, in turn, emboldens the Christian along the way to find grounds for commitment, faith, active love, compassion, and joy.

Christian pessimism may be a way of theologically framing the reality of AIDS in terms of the "Answer" of the cross to which I referred in the Preface of this book. The realism of the cross offers a framework for interpreting the suffering of AIDS itself. But can we go further? Can we learn anything from the example of a Francis, who did not hold the leper at arm's length, but embraced him, kissed his wounds, and thus let the leper free Francis himself? What we have in the example of Francis is the penetration of another's world, and letting that world into our own, leading to the point of conversion. If a source of suffering such as AIDS demands to be interpreted by theology, could the sorrow and even mystery of this disease, and other forms of massive human suffering, in some way inform our theology, or perhaps our theologizing, if we were to allow it to do so? The implications for theology are rich.

AIDS as reality and as metaphor urges a theology that consciously serves the pastoral mission of the Church because systematic theology and Christian spirituality work out of the common ground of the real, both seen and unseen. They cannot begin with the Answer to such a massive mystery of suffering; they must begin with the crisis itself: the real. Such a theology will not rest content with grounding expressions for pastoral compassion while holding the human reality that has evoked these calls at arm's length. Rather, it will invite a form of theologizing that asks us to be attentive to reality, reverential in the face of the truth that it discloses, intellectually reflective upon this truth, and prayerful, discerning, and loving in our response to the human condition it represents.[31] It could force a revisiting and even revision of some cherished ways of framing theological approaches to sin, suffering, and death, as well as the experience of God in relation to the unfolding of human experience in our time, including shifting understandings of human sexuality. This need has already become clear in the realm of moral theology, where the realities of AIDS, especially in relation to human sexuality, have forced a review of some theological positions developed before the advent of this disease and before the changes in sexual consciousness and patterns of sexuality that have taken place in recent years throughout the world.

AIDS is a contemporary leper's bell for theology. Like other massive calamities, it pushes us toward fresh approaches to the foundational narrative of faith, that of Jesus himself, as it works in dialectical relationship with the continual outpouring of the "data" of human experience. In view of this fact, then, we might ask whether theology is not being called upon to play the part of Francis on the road, recognizing that often enough the way to a deeper apprehension of God is a direction far different from the one we want to take.[32] For there is much to fear on the road of the lepers. But if the story of Jesus tells us anything, it is that this direction, the way of the leper, is the way to the God of empathy who wills to share in our lot. And the cross is the supreme symbol of that empathy.

Chapter Five

The Other Side of the Tapestry

*I have a feeling that there exist for you in this earthly life, perhaps
because you have been called more than any other to catch a glimpse
of the other side of the tapestry, certain very dark and dangerous
problems.*[1]
　　　　　　　　　　　　　　　—Jacques Maritain to Julien Green

EMPATHY, YES. But what happens when empathy seems absent?
What happens when the cross itself does not seem to stand as
a symbol of hope, but rather of more suffering, a suffering seemingly
required of some people because of their lot in life? Some people
afflicted with AIDS, especially those who are homosexual, have seen
themselves before the cross in this way.

We turn now to a matter that concerns many who are both Catholic and homosexual: the attempt to assimilate into their lives the
teaching of the Roman Magisterium on homosexuality, and in particular the incorporation of the cross into their sexual identities and
lives. For in the face of the existence of Catholics whose sexual orientation is homosexual, the Church currently offers a stark spiritual
counsel: to join one's sufferings, whatever those may be precisely as a
homosexual person, to the sufferings of Jesus on the cross and to live
a life of sexual renunciation. In proposing the cross as the appropriate
emblem of spiritual aspiration for gay[2] Catholics, Roman teaching explicitly links the state of finding oneself to be homosexual with trial
and difficulty and thus recommends a lived spirituality of the cross
focused on a blending of the sufferings attendant upon this condition
with the passion of Christ. As the first English version of the *Catechism of the Catholic Church* stated: "The number of men and women

104

who have deep-seated homosexual tendencies is not negligible. They do not choose their homosexual condition; for most of them it is a trial. . . . These persons are called to fulfill God's will in their lives and, if they are Christians, to unite to the sacrifice of the Lord's cross the difficulties they may encounter from their condition."[3]

This congruence in religious imagination of homosexuality and suffering in the symbol of the cross was foreshadowed in the correspondence between Jacques Maritain and the French-American writer Julien Green in the first half of the past century, well before definitive Vatican pronouncements on the matter. Green later described these years, before he finally renounced sex altogether, as an impediment to God, as his own "crucifixion" on the cross of sex.[4] In what was clearly a painful admission of the fact that he had not been fully honest about himself in a conversation with Maritain, Green, who had been struggling for years with his homosexuality, alludes to his sexual state by admitting to Maritain: "You asked me if I intended to live alone and I said yes when I should have said no."[5] Maritain, who had many close gay friends, responded with pathos verging on alarm.

> Let me speak to you frankly: a conversation like the one we had, a letter like the one I received this morning, casts me down before God and makes me ask for death. Because God has led me to understand I *must* help souls like yours to work out the problems in which they find themselves involved.[6]

Yet it is worth noting that Maritain expresses his empathy for the state that Green endures:

> I will never judge you. I do not think you are living in sin. I know nothing about that. What I do know is the depth of your heart, and that you are inclined, as a matter of fact, to push scrupulosity too far, and that at no price would you wish to offend Jesus. And because of this very fact, what causes you pain causes me even deeper pain. I have a feeling that there exist for you in this earthly life, perhaps because you have been

called more than any other to catch a glimpse of the other side of the tapestry, certain very dark and dangerous problems.[7]

He then offered what he considered the only solution to the conflict between the imprisonments of the flesh and the ends of religion: sexual abstinence for the love of God:

> What makes everything so serious is that it is a question of our debt to Uncreated Love. The Gospel nowhere tells us to mutilate our hearts, but it counsels us to make ourselves eunuchs for the Kingdom of God. This is how I think the question must be posed.

And, lest there be any doubt about his position, he based his counsel to Green on the ideal of a "white" marriage between a man and a woman, a separation of love from the flesh, lived as a kind of participation in the sacrifice of the cross of Christ:

> I know some married couples who for the love of Christ have made a vow of continence, and whose mutual love has divinely deepened because of it. Why could the same *separation* not be possible in other cases? Or must we put down the Cross of Christ and replace it with the cross of own choice?[8]

Much later, and before Green's attempted renunciation of sex, Maritain pointed to the example of Max Jacob, the French Jewish surrealist poet and convert to Catholicism who eventually died of natural causes at Drancy, the Nazi camp outside of Paris. Maritain writes:

> Max Jacob died a saint. Can we not believe that he showed us the only true solution to the problem [of the flesh and religion] when it takes its most painful forms? Max went to confession every day and to Communion every day. . . . Max found the way, and was, more than anyone else, simply pushed to the extreme. To have recourse to these two sacraments each day, as he did, demands a kind of heroic, but not impossible will; there is no problem stronger than God.[9]

It is remarkable how close Maritain comes to the position that eventually became formally stated in Catholic doctrine, including the full extent of sexual renunciation in fulfillment of the cross of Christ.

Yet I want to suggest that if we wish to find a route to the cross that leads to hope, indeed to joy, we must do so from a reconsideration of the suffering attendant upon human sexuality, whether it be labeled gay or not. Sexuality, whatever its mode of lived existence, entails some psychic and spiritual suffering, as Julien Green's life surely attested. But Maritain himself was to observe that there is a distinction to be made between the love proper to friendship, and the love that transcends creaturely human limits, what Maritain, following Raïssa, calls a "mad, boundless love for God" that results in a state of contemplation. The road to this love must pass through what he calls "love-passion" or romantic love, then through the "authentic love" that involves some real suffering.[10] For, as Maritain clearly knew, sexuality entails more than biological function: it is at once biological, psychological, and spiritual — hence defying reduction to theologies based on sexual acts or even to the exclusive end of human reproduction. We need to be freed from a certain biological and metaphysical essentialism found in some theologizing about sexuality, a tendency to reduce sexuality and even personal identity to sex acts, sexual or gender identity, biological gender constructs, or metaphorical and idealist theologies of complementarity built on these premises. Any counsel of the cross in regard to gay people must take into account the complex reality of human sexuality itself, and somehow relate it to the Love toward which creaturely love and passion ultimately lead.

The Counsel of the Cross for Homosexual Catholics

The founding spirit of the Church's counsel of the cross for gay Catholics is found in a 1986 document entitled "Letter to All Catholic Bishops on the Pastoral Care of Homosexual Persons" (*Homosexualitatis problema*).[11] Published by the Congregation for the Doctrine of the Faith, this document states:

Fundamentally, [homosexuals] are called to enact the will of God in their life by joining whatever sufferings and difficulties they experience in virtue of their condition to the sacrifice of the Lord's Cross. That Cross, for the believer, is a fruitful sacrifice since from that death come life and redemption. While any call to carry the cross or to understand a Christian's suffering in this way will predictably be met with bitter ridicule by some, it should be remembered that this is the way to eternal life for all who follow Christ.

In an unusually pointed usage of Scripture, the document then applies the words of Galatians specifically to the situation of gay persons:

It is, in effect, none other than the teaching of Paul the Apostle to the Galatians when he says that the Spirit produces in the lives of the faithful "love, joy, peace, patience, kindness, goodness, trustfulness, gentleness, and self-control" (5:22) and further (v. 24), "You cannot belong to Christ unless you crucify all self-indulgent passions and desires."

But self-denial is not an end in itself. According to this teaching, it is for the homosexual person the path toward liberation from vice and salvation of one's soul. The document continues:

... The Cross is a denial of self, but in service to the will of God himself who makes life come from death and empowers those who trust in him to practice virtue in place of vice.

To celebrate the Paschal Mystery, it is necessary to let that Mystery become imprinted in the fabric of daily life. To refuse to sacrifice one's own will in obedience to the will of the Lord is effectively to prevent salvation. Just as the Cross was central to the expression of God's redemptive love for us in Jesus, so the conformity of the self-denial of homosexual men and women with the sacrifice of the Lord will constitute for them a source of self-giving which will save them from a way of life which constantly threatens to destroy them.

The next sentence reads:

> Christians who are homosexual are called, as all of us are, to
> a chaste life. As they dedicate their lives to understanding the
> nature of God's personal call to them, they will be able to cele-
> brate the Sacrament of Penance more faithfully and receive
> the Lord's grace so freely offered there in order to convert their
> lives more fully to his Way.

While penance is mentioned here as of aid to gay persons in attaining
a chaste life, no mention is made of the graces accruing from one's
baptism or from the life of the Eucharist. Maritain, by contrast, points
to Max Jacob's daily frequenting of the Eucharist as well as Penance
as aids toward chastity.

Nevertheless, as this document correctly states, the self-denial of
the Cross is a spiritual counsel offered to all Christians. It has been
proffered to generations of Christians in helping them to face, within
the context of faith, the sufferings of the human lot. According to
this spiritual counsel, identification with the cross of Christ can lead
to a life lived in accord with the will of God rather than enslavement
to one's own desires. It can purify people of the desire to have control
over all aspects of their lives, and of the evil tendencies which give
rise to sin. For all Christians, the Paschal Mystery is made real partly
to the degree that it is made one's own in a personal way. The Gospel
frequently states that self-denial is the necessary precondition to
discipleship (cf. Matt. 10:39, Luke 17:33). The Gospel also counsels
that it is necessary to bear one's own cross (Matt. 10:38). Paul's
theology is imbued with a sense of the cross, so that only in the cross
of Christ might one boast (Gal. 6:14). Hebrews sets forth Jesus as an
example of one who endured the cross of life (Heb. 12:2), and as such
stands as a pioneer in faith. And, as we noted earlier, Christian devo-
tional and mystical literature, notably that inspired by *The Imitation
of Christ*, recommends the cross as the pathway to the perfection of
the Kingdom. This counsel was convincingly put forth by Pope John
Paul II in the apostolic letter *Salvifici Doloris* where the Pope laid
out a phenomenology of suffering and a theology of the cross where
every person "is also called to share in that suffering through which

the Redemption was accomplished." For, "In bringing about the Redemption through suffering, Christ has also raised human suffering to the level of the Redemption. Thus each man [sic], in his suffering, can also become a sharer in the redemptive suffering of Christ."[12]

So this spiritual counsel is native to Christian soil. But questions arise when it is specified for gay people in particular. As it appears in *Homosexualitatis problema,* the counsel of the cross makes several assumptions about homosexuality itself. Among these are: that the sufferings of the homosexual attend his or her "condition," a word which suggests that this state is not a chosen orientation; that the passions and desires that may emanate from the homosexual condition, to the degree that they are voluntary, and certainly if acted upon, are self-indulgent and should be "crucified"; that homosexuality as a condition intrinsically tends toward vice and death; that gay people who have not sacrificed their wills in a pursuit of nonsexual chastity are constantly threatened by destruction, presumably their own self-destruction, and eternal loss; and that chastity for the gay Catholic means sexual abstinence — presumably to be distinguished from the call to celibacy, though perhaps tending toward that ideal.

These assumptions, in turn, lead to a rather complex understanding of the cross in relation to gay Catholic existence, and raise several questions for us here.

First, the sheer fact of being gay, which is said to involve so much trial and difficulty, is a mode of participation in the sufferings of Christ, one which presumably is instrumental in bringing about Christ's saving work, thus saving a gay person from perdition. The "trials" of the homosexual condition find a kind of likeness with the passion of Jesus on the cross. By joining one's trials as a gay person to the sufferings of Jesus on the cross, one will find an identification with Jesus. But why, one might ask, should this identification with Jesus issue specifically from the suffering that attends one's sexual constitution? What precisely are the trials and difficulties in question, and what are their sources? Is there perhaps an overly particular rhetorical association here of the "trials" of gay Catholics with the Passion of Jesus Christ?[13]

Second, through the self-denial of sexual renunciation, one enters into a fruitful self-sacrifice, thus crucifying one's sexuality, as it were, and overcoming the tendencies that lead to objectively grave evil. The weight of this assumption leads to the conclusion that the effects of homosexuality as a given state tending toward so much evil must be overcome, and can only be overcome through heroic self-denial (what Maritain understood as the crucifixion of the effects of this condition), and that by implication this is the only road to salvation for the gay Catholic. This road is marked by uniting the plight of one's sexual condition to the suffering and sacrifice of Jesus on the cross, emulating Jesus in his own self-denial precisely through a renunciation of sex, and through this mode of imitating Christ, overcoming the power of evil inherent in one's intrinsically disordered sexual condition. One thus aspires toward a state of "Christian perfection."[14] In view of such a teaching, we are led to ask whether the counsel of the cross, as presented here, is an expression of faith that could positively lead a gay person to a life of faith-filled hope, or whether this is merely a theological default position, which is the only logical conclusion to be derived from the presupposition that the homosexual condition is intrinsically disordered.

Third, one can find in the sacrifice of Jesus on the cross a pattern of self-giving which will in itself save one from the constant threat of self-destruction. The view of the cross implicit here is that it represents the "fruitful sacrifice" of self which eventually results in a life of self-donation, giving to others. This counsel is certainly apt for all Christians, not only for gays, and is in fact the foundation for an understanding of Christian love in the teaching of Jesus.[15] But can this teaching of Jesus be tied so directly to the "problem" of homosexuality? Does this specificity of application, and its underlying emphasis on avoiding eternal loss, miss something central to the dynamic of love revealed on the cross itself — a suffering love that is freely accepted and leads toward life?

To summarize: The official teaching of the Church for gay Catholics offers a spirituality of the cross that would symbolize a participation in the sufferings of Christ. These sufferings, as a means of cooperation with God's grace, would gradually help to transform the sufferer into a state approximating if not even reaching perfection in the practice of chaste sexual abstinence, a kind of catharsis from the burden of the condition itself. Participation in the cross would therefore prevent the intrinsic direction of this sexuality from reaching its finality, in sin and death. The cross of Christ is not a path one chooses out of freedom alone; it is in a sense the only route for one who is beset by the paradox of a sexuality that is at once a part of God's creation yet intrinsically disordered, for it establishes the bearer of that condition as a person with a tendency toward evil. The path of the cross is fortified by the sacraments, especially Penance. And perhaps like the unchosen condition of homosexuality itself, which for some is the only way they can be, the path of the cross is the only route through Christian life for the gay Catholic. It is the cross of a necessary asceticism that leads, through an act of obedience, toward a transcendent form of loving.

What Manner of Suffering?

The Roman Magisterium is not incorrect when it says that suffering attends the homosexual condition. For example, there is no question that throughout the world homosexual persons continue to encounter prejudice, even against their persons and not only with respect to the sexual acts they might or might not engage in. The fate of Matthew Shepherd, a gay youth murdered in Wyoming in a crucifixion-like slaying, looms as a symbol in its own right of where this kind of prejudice can lead. And there are many subtler forms of suffering that attend being gay in both society and within the Church. There is notably the struggle involved in finding oneself a Catholic who is gay and trying to make sense of and live with a teaching that declares one's inclination to be intrinsically ordered toward evil. Moral theologian Stephen J. Pope has noted "the pain and suffering heaped on gay people for millennia"[16] and that

> the Magisterium's message about gay sexual orientation is powerfully stigmatizing and dehumanizing. It is also at least tacitly, if not explicitly, liable to be used to support exactly

the kinds of unjust discrimination that the Church has re-
peatedly condemned. Describing someone's sexual identity as
"gravely disordered" would seem to arouse suspicion, mistrust,
and alienation. This conclusion is reinforced by the painful
direct psychological experience of many gay people.[17]

Michele Dillon puts it this way: gay and lesbian Catholics must
perforce learn to own their Catholic identities differently.[18]

And several writers have pointed to the particular paradox of
clergy in the Catholic Church who are of homosexual orientation
and who find themselves living within the bounds of an institutional
teaching which they are called upon to represent and to which they
cannot readily give a full assent of intellect and will. One of the more
balanced treatments of this topic comes from Donald Cozzens:

> Most gay priests, I believe, live with another level of pain and
> conflict that is only minimally understood, even by their families
> and friends. Their church teaches that a homosexual orienta-
> tion is an objective disorder. Does that mean the church holds
> that they *as persons* are objectively disordered? No, but this fine
> distinction is of little comfort from an existential point of view.
> Can objectively disordered people be really holy? Lead lives of
> genuine sanctity? Without question, but sexual identity is so
> central to a fundamental sense of self that it is an easy step to
> conclude that a gay individual himself or herself is "objectively
> disordered. . . . " As men of the church, they are expected to
> uphold this teaching and bring it to the attention of the gay
> and lesbian parishioners they counsel.[19]

Then, too, beyond the inner struggles of homosexual priests, there
are the forms of suffering that attend unrequited and frustrated desires brought on by the inability of various familial, social, cultural,
and religious structures to accept the fact that some people wish
to express love for a person of the same gender. Eugene Kennedy
even describes the effect of such negative judgments as sinful, making people feel "guilty, as charged, of being human."[20] It is indeed a
profound form of suffering to be rejected by those who claim their

love, to experience another's denial of one's ownmost reality, much less the seemingly natural validity of that which lies in the recesses of one's psyche. Ultimately, it can seem that such rejection and denial is a denial of one's very person, of one's existence *as* the person that they are, for sexuality, including both physiological attractions and self-identity, is an inalienable part, one of the many parts of what it means to be the person that one finds oneself to be.

Beyond rejection and denial by family and friends, there is also, of course, the phenomenon of socially sanctioned prejudice against gay people either because they are homosexual in their private lives, or claim to be gay as a public part of their identity as persons. And to the degree that Vatican teaching insists on the inherent dignity of all human persons, regardless of their sexual constitution, this sin of prejudice and judgment is recognized and condemned. Catholic Church teaching frequently refers to the dignity of persons, gay or otherwise, that must be safeguarded. On the other hand, Vatican teaching also makes a distinction between "just" and "unjust" discrimination. Stephen Pope concludes:

> The magisterium's treatment of the issue of discrimination replicates the confusions and ambiguities of its treatment of the dignity of gay people. The magisterium, and especially the Congregation for the Doctrine of the Faith, presents an important substantive principle that disallows unjust discrimination but then undercuts its own credibility by failing to register its understanding of the full extent to which discrimination against gays persists as a social evil.[21]

All of these forms of prejudice against gay and lesbian people, some of them imbedded in the teaching of the Magisterium itself, are sources of deep suffering for many gay and lesbian people.

Latent in Vatican teaching is the assumption that a gay person must be in anguish simply because they are gay and that this condition is contrary to nature. It cannot but lead to great internal suffering, albeit unspecified by the magisterium itself. Some gay people do indeed suffer, as we have noted. But what this teaching does not address is the fact that sexuality itself — whether hetero-sexual or homosexual — entails suffering, the perpetual sense of the unattainability of a good, a kind of loss. For sexuality involves the interplay between the most ardent drives toward transcendence, and the strongest desires toward interpersonal communion, both of which are difficult if not impossible of a final attainment. What Roman teaching does not address, therefore, are the ways in which human sexuality itself leads to suffering in a deeply spiritual sense.

In order to pursue this line of thought, I turn to one of Paul Ri-coeur's writings on sexuality. In a short essay, "Wonder, Eroticism, and Enigma," Ricoeur offers what might be some of the most helpful pre-theological reflection on the suffering entailed in human sex-uality, both heterosexual and homosexual.[22] Sexuality is reducible neither to the pursuit of pleasure alone, the erotic, nor to its "tech-nical" ends, procreation and generativity. When reduced to the erotic alone, it becomes eroti*cism,* "a restless desire for pleasure," and an existential problem, for "it dissociates itself from the network of ten-dencies linked by the concern for a lasting, intense, and intimate interpersonal bond. . . ."[23] But it cannot be confined to instrumen-tal ends, such as procreation, nor only to its institutional sanctions, such as marriage or celibacy. Sexuality resists containment. Why is this the case?

First, Ricoeur says, because sexuality is bound up with Eros, sexu-ality is pre-linguistic. It is a power that precedes thought. "It mobilizes language, true, but it crosses it, jostles it, sublimates it, stupefies it, pulverizes it into a murmur, an invocation. Sexuality . . . is Eros and not Logos."[24] Therefore, our attempts to represent it or even to con-tain it within our various language games and, indeed, theological constructs, are constantly challenged by the rather irrational, alogical character of sexuality that lies at its very heart.

Second, because Eros belongs to the "pre-technical" domains of human existence, sexuality cannot be reduced to "technical" ends, such as procreation. Of course sexual relations can lead to the gen-eration of new life, and new life "by nature" comes from sexual relations. But the point is that even when viewed from this per-spective, or when "controlled" through techniques such as various methods of birth control or, more generally, social mores governing sexual intercourse within marriage, sexuality "remains basically foreign to the 'intention-tool-thing' relationship. . . . The body to body relationship — or better, person to flesh to flesh to person — remains basically non-technical."[25] This implies, for Ricoeur, that arguments about sexuality that would correlate it with technical ends, such as the ends of nature, do not necessarily inhere within sexuality itself. Rather, for Ricoeur, these belong principally to the realm of interpretation, not to an ontology inscribed by or in nature, nor to a divine or cosmic pattern. As many moral theologians have argued, sexuality itself challenges the adequacy of some versions of natural law, notably those that are geared to upholding exclusively the procreative ends of the sexual organs.

Third, Eros, which is bound up with human sexuality, cannot be reduced to a sexual "act" or even to any particular institutional arrangement. This is not to argue against the religiously, culturally, and socially prescribed nature of monogamous marriage between a man and a woman, but to suggest that even this holy institution is subject to the volatility of Eros: " . . . [W]hatever one may say of its equilibrium in marriage, Eros is not institutional. One offends it by reducing it to a contract, to a conjugal duty."[26] The illogic of the erotic within sexuality in fact stands as a threat to the desired stability of the institution of marriage itself. The only "law" governing Eros is "the reciprocity of gift." When sexuality is viewed not as gift, but as an institutionalized life contract ratified by a consummated sexual act (the marital act, duty, obligation, debt), then we have lost sight of something prior to these interpretations, something that cannot be evaded even within the institution of marriage itself: the uncontainable, restless quality of human sexuality that threatens cherished discourses, theologies, and institutions that we have constructed around it. These considerations constitute what Ricoeur calls the "enigma of sexuality" — a tension within sexuality that eludes resolution.

Yet, he argues, the power of Eros within human sexuality need not result in eroticism, the triumph of the egoistic pursuit of pleasure over the ideal of mutual interpersonal exchange, and deep interpersonal bond. The countervailing power to eroticism is tenderness, which can also result from the powers of Eros itself. But this tenderness as a modality and a finality of sexuality is always threatened, internally, by the possibility of eroticism per se. And it is this very possibility that is the cause of suffering within the sexual domain of human existence. Sexuality exists in this ongoing tension between Eros threatening to become eroticism, and the desire of human beings for transcendence in and through bodily bonding and tenderness, also the works of Eros.

The issue at hand, therefore, is where Eros finally tends. Here I would agree with Sarah Coakley, who argues that the erotic denotes not only the desires of the human heart, ultimately for a union with God, but also of "God's proto-erotic desire for us."[27] Perhaps the deepest form of sexual suffering is the frustration of this divine desire, the unrequited love of God for human beings and of human beings for God, which finds its form within the enigma of the erotic itself, in the desire to give and receive a love that is divine. This unrequitedness is itself a form of the absence of a good (if not of its very loss), of a good hoped for but not yet held (or, if once held, perhaps now lost). It is a form of suffering, in the form of the absence of a good, or a good not yet finally attained.

Embracing the Cross

It is at this point that we can turn to consideration of a more em-bracing counsel of the cross for gay, and all, Christians. Here again we turn to Karl Rahner. As we saw in the last chapter, for Rahner, the cross stands not as a symbol of asceticism only, but as a symbol of both God's own incomprehensible love for us in the death of Jesus Christ and our own call to embrace it. Embracing the cross implies that the cross entails following Jesus crucified in one's whole life, but it also entails assuming a posture of gratitude toward the cross mani-fested in love for others, through a living self-denial that comes from the positive experience of God's grace as one begifted by God.

The following of Christ crucified signals more than suffering in and with Jesus on the cross, although that kind of piety is certainly not rejected, and is in fact embraced by Rahner:

Christianity forbids us to reach for an analgesic in such a way that we are no longer willing to drink the chalice of the death of this existence with Jesus Christ.... [I]t is only when we live out this pessimistic realism and renounce every ideology which absolutizes a particular sector of human existence and makes it an idol, it is only then that it is possible for us to allow God to give us the hope which really makes us free.[28]

But the cross signifies yet more: a posture toward life that sees death as the final limit, and Jesus as the trailblazer of that path through his own suffering and death. In John's Gospel, Jesus' death on the cross is only formally distinguishable from his glorification in the resurrection. Rahner moves this Johannine insight front and center. The suffering and self-sacrifice of the cross, though inescapable and essential, is not an end in itself for Christian life, nor the trump card for faith. As we have seen, the suffering of the cross is the path to resurrection.[29] Following Christ crucified therefore implies that all Christians, not just certain selected ones (the poor or degraded, or various minorities, including gays), have as a central part of their Christian vocation a consciousness of their own death, and of their heading toward it and through it. Jesus set his face like flint toward Jerusalem, toward his death and glorious destiny; so, too, the Christian, any and all Christians. The cross is not the preserve only of a tragically afflicted caste. All Christians are "elected"[30] to the destiny of glory through the cross, even in and through their sexuality. Borrowing from Ricoeur, we might say that there is a sense in which the divine proto-erotic love leads to the cross, in a love that suffers in order to give of itself.

The fundamental Christian response to the cross is one of gratitude because it is in the cross that God's love is revealed. Rahner admits that it is difficult to see in the suffering and death of the cross how precisely we are loved by God, especially in the face of our own sinfulness, and the cumulative effect of the many sins that lead to the cross ("the death-dealing revelation of sin which inflicts a terrible paroxysm on God himself who came into the world in order to destroy death by his own death"). But it is precisely here that we also encounter "the ineffable outpouring of his love which did not hesitate to sustain sin and death. Out of death and love"[31] there has come such grace. And so, in the face of this, the Christian posture is one of a gratitude that, with the help of God's grace, leads to a self-abandonment to that same love that was revealed on the cross.

Rahner's formulation balances both dimensions of the Cross — its darkness and its revelatory power — without finally explaining it away or reducing it to a spirituality only for a particular set of abject souls. All are called to a courage that leads to joining in the sufferings of Christ on the cross. Indeed, Rahner's final positive rendering of the concupiscence of human nature is as " . . . the form *in* which the Christian experiences Christ's sufferings and suffers them himself to the end."[32]

But to what end? What kind of asceticism does this lead to? First, there is definitely a place for the "carrying of one's cross" in this theology, for we cannot rid ourselves of the crosses of this existence, the imprisonments of our finite natures. The question is the posture, the attitude, with which we face this fact:

> No one can rid himself of the cross of this existence. But precisely for this reason it is difficult to know whether we accept this cross in faith, hope and love to our salvation, or whether we only bear it protesting secretly, because we cannot free ourselves from it but are nailed to it like the robber on the left of Jesus, who cursed his fate and blasphemed the crucified Lord by his side.[33]

While Christian sexual existence does entail sacrifice, self-denial, and transformation, it can also embrace a love that is fundamentally life-affirming and virtue-building. In this balancing of both dimensions of the cross lies the "demand" of Christian asceticism:

> This affirmation and demand are incomprehensible. Gratitude for the cross is certainly anything but a self-evident possibility. That we accept bravely and without self-pity the harshness that is a part of life together with its vitality, strength, and glory, is a demanding aspect of life that is by no means easy.[34]

How we go about this, and in what spirit of renunciation, remains to be determined:

> When do we accept it? Certainly not if we talk much about it and imagine ourselves very brave. Certainly not by exaggerating the little sorrows of our daily life and whining and whimpering about them. Certainly not if we imagine that the will to bear the cross prevents us from defending ourselves and from leading a free, healthy and sound life as long as it is at all possible.[35]

Specifically, this leads to a Christian asceticism that stresses the sacrifice of "positive values and goods of this world"[36] rather than the avoidance of what is deemed evil a priori. The latter approach tends toward a form of latter-day Manichaeism, stressing a flight from the world and seeing the world, and creation as God has wrought it, even in its variety, as something to be avoided as tainted with evil. Renunciation of nature as it is given in the name of renunciation of evil can hardly comport with a spirituality of the cross rooted in gratitude and desire to follow in the way of Jesus. On the contrary, we could fall into "a pseudo-ethical or pseudo-religious paroxysm of sacrifice which is not willed by God and which is basically not a real loving surrender to God's will."[37] Such could in the end become an act of despair, because it would not be the response to an invitation so much as an act of sheer will, hope against hope, which can only dissolve into hopelessness.

Further, the asceticism of renunciation, even of sexual renunciation in the evangelical counsels, can only come from a positive call by God as the result of a "believing gesture of love which reaches out beyond the world and its goods, even those of a personal nature." Rahner continues:

> The fact *that* one may understand renunciation as an expression of such a shift of existence can of course be explained only by a positive (general and individual) call by God, and this in view of the fact that even positive acts can be sanctified and hence renunciation cannot in any sense be called the sole possible

form of realization of transcending love . . . God must give his special and express permission for this going beyond the world.[38]

While it is true that a Catholic understanding of faith includes the mediation of God's intentions through the teaching and life of the Church itself, the call to this particular kind of asceticism is a call that can come only from God. The Church can only mediate that call, particularly through the sacraments. Sexual renunciation as response to an authentic call by God, as in the evangelical counsels (vows of religious life), belongs to the final, eschatological, character of the Church as the Body of Christ in history, and is a realization of that character, particularly in and through the sacraments of Baptism and Eucharist.[39] It is not a state that one can execute with any success by a sheer act of will, nor through resignation to the implications of fate or to a sense that one is simply imprisoned in one's sexuality.

In relation to this, and as we have noted in what is lacking in Vatican teaching on homosexuality, special attention should be directed toward the Eucharist. In Rahner's essay, "The Eucharist and Suffering,"[40] he explains how the sufferings of Christ flow into the life of the Christian through the Eucharist in a three-fold modality: as the sacrifice of Christ for us, as the means of God's self-communication in grace, and as an intimate binding within the mystical Body of Christ. All three of these modalities emphasize God's movement toward the person of faith. Participation in the sufferings of Christ are realized by virtue of the initiative of Christ towards us, even in the sufferings God allows us. It is not our place to "count" our sufferings and to join them, as it were, to the sufferings of Christ:

No, the measure of suffering appointed to us is God's disposing; it happens in accordance with the wise and inscrutable decrees of the one Spirit of God who distributes even these gifts of grace to the individual members of the Body of Christ, as he wills (cf. 1 Cor. 12:11). And this Spirit gives also the strength to bear each cross; together with the weakness of Christ, his strength also comes to dwell in us, and our weakness is given to us only so that God's strength may be perfected in us (2 Cor. 12:9 sq.).[41]

There is a concern here to avoid the tendency to take it upon one-self to chart the way toward participation in the Passion of Christ. This is a matter of grace, not of one's own doing. The distribution of God's graces, including the dark graces that come through suffering, cannot be manipulated, much less possessed. They come to us, especially in the climate of the Eucharist. Rahner notes that while it is true according to Paul that we have been appointed to suffering (1 Thess. 3:3), and "that suffering and death are essential characteristics of Christian existence as such, necessary consequences and living manifestations of our being in Christ by grace," the Eucharist is the sacrament of the constant growth and maturing of this life of grace. He continues:

> ... it is the sacrament which is meant to ensure that we live more and more "in Him" and become ever more like Him. Must not the Holy Eucharist then draw us ever more deeply also into the mystery of the Cross of Christ? ... The Eucharist, moreover, renews the memory of the sufferings of Christ *even by letting Christ's sufferings flow over to us together with grace.*[42]

We note here the dynamic of participation in the sufferings of Christ: the sufferings of Christ are granted to any of us as part of the flow of grace towards us. This is not something we ask for or take upon ourselves.

Finally, a properly *Christian* asceticism will lead to love of God and neighbor. But an asceticism of the cross that focuses only on an individual's combat with the flesh, and final victory over all of its unruliness, paints only part of the picture of a virtuous life, and arguably not the most important part. If a Christian wishes to grow ever more deeply Christian as such, following the crucified, then this would, by the logic of faith, lead to a deeper sense of love both for God and one's fellow human beings — a movement away from oneself, to be sure, and toward one's involvement in the wider sphere of God's creation. Christian asceticism of the cross leads to a spirit of empathy, of one for another. It is modeled on God's own empathic entry into the world of human suffering in the person of Jesus, one who took on all forms of human suffering, including the burden of the sin of the world, endured them himself, and redeemed them. It is further modeled on Jesus' own free acceptance of God's empathy, even in his own sufferings, manifest not only on the cross itself, but in the patterns of his life. The cross, though, stands as the climax of this life, the place where the divine empathy is both given and received, and so the cross stands at the heart of a human-divine love that is first reflected in the human-divine reality of Jesus. This divine empathy, manifest in the empathy of Jesus for all, entails suffering for those other than oneself, the expression of a divine empathy. It is here that one's own suffering in the paradoxes of gay Catholic existence begin to make sense: an asceticism built on an embrace of the divine empathy, leading to a life of tenderness and self-giving love, or kenosis (Phil. 2:1–11).

The sufferings of the gay person can, in fact, lead that person beyond a stance of victimhood toward a stance of uncanny empathy for those who suffer but who might not have a clue about the suffering of the gay person, because they have never known it first hand. Alternatively, the sexual suffering of the married couple struggling to live through years of fidelity, or of the divorced Catholic who feels estranged from herself because of her estrangement from the Church, could lead to an empathy for the sense of paradox lived out by many gay Catholics. It strikes me that this kind of empathy is in keeping with a positively interpreted theology of the cross, one in which the Christian enters willingly into the crucible of life, through love. It is not simply a theology of self-denial based on the assumption that one's inclinations are not only disordered, but essentially self-indulgent.

Such a theology of empathy, could also lead to a deeper understanding of the Paschal Mystery as the empathy of God, an empathy into which God invites all Christians *qua* Christian, by virtue of their common baptism. This is the empathy of the divine entry into the pathos of human existence in a tender way. This manifestation of divine empathy in the Paschal Mystery of Christ could also open up the theological imagination of the Church's teachers toward other ways of imagining human sexuality and, more broadly, human nature, which is, after all, originally established through and in God's self-revelation in the God-Man Jesus Christ. We could move beyond the dehumanizing effects of reducing sexuality to the human body and its functions, or of reducing human nature to sexual identity, and open up its symbolic value as an icon of the divine tenderness.

Seen in this way, gay Catholic existence could be approached, not simply as a conundrum, a *problem*, something standing in the way of the truth of the Gospel, but rather as an invitation to a different way of looking at things, and toward a deeper embrace of that Gospel which threatens to subvert some of our most cherished notions about our God whose name is Love.

Part Three

Living in Hope

Chapter Six

A Cross That Leads to Hope

Putting oneself at the service of the resurrection means working continually, often against hope, in the service of eschatological ideals: justice, peace, solidarity, the life of the weak, community, dignity. . . . And these partial "resurrections" can generate hope in the final resurrection, the conviction that God did indeed perform the impossible, gave life to one crucified and will give life to all the crucified.[1]

— Jon Sobrino

WE NOW TURN to that dimension of the Christian imagination that looks toward the future, God's future, from the standpoint of present human reality: eschatology. Eschatology, derives from the Greek *eschaton,* for the end, and sets a horizon of hope against which all the dark suffering of human existence must be set. The Psalmist sings, "At the end of the sky is the rising of the sun" (Psalm 31). The cross is silhouetted against a sky that promises the break of dawn. A theology of the cross has to include a focus not only on the stark reality evoked by the symbol of the cross itself, but also the sources of hope that attend the cross in Christian imagination. This includes the relationship between the cross and the incarnation and the resurrection, between both the hope-filled divine entrance into human life, and the final victory of God's love over suffering and death. The cross leads to a focus on the full reality of enfleshed human life, not only my own, but what I share with others; and the destiny of this life, reached through solidarity with others in sharing the human lot. In the end, a theology of the cross offers an eschatology, an understanding of the finality of things in God, which is deeply hopeful in both its origins and its fulfillment. In light of what I have discussed thus far in this book, I will propose here a spirituality of the cross that might lead to a sense of hope in the midst of life's suffering.

The vehicle I propose for developing such a theology of the cross, one that will also lead to a spirituality of the cross, is the imagination of St. Ignatius of Loyola and of the Jesuit spiritual tradition. This is the spiritual tradition that so deeply influenced Rahner and many other Jesuit theologians as well. Perhaps more than the various other spiritualities available to Christians, the Ignatian imagination offers an eschatology that is not other-worldly, or pitched in a heavenly future. Rather, transcendent reality, and human hope in God's future, are found within the teeming reality of human beings here on earth, in the depths of their sufferings as well as their joys. At the center of this eschatological drama stands the cross. In order to see this, we turn to Jesuit Rome.

The Cross at the Center of Ignatian Imagination

On the ancient site of the Temple of Isis in the city of Rome stands the Church of San Ignazio, a church originally intended for completion in 1640 for the centenary anniversary of the founding of the Society of Jesus. The church was to serve as the chapel of the already fabled Roman College, an institutional embodiment of Jesuit ideals in both humanistic education in the post-Reformation era and missionary activity for the Catholic faith in the newly colonized worlds of America and Asia. As such, it was to be a glorious monument to the genius of the founder of the Jesuits and an illustration of his expansive religious vision. The imposing facade of this new temple, a somewhat cleaner version of the Gesù Church nearby, comes suddenly into view as one meanders through the narrow streets in back of the Roman College and, passing through a thin opening, comes upon the salon-like baroque Piazza of San Ignazio, which has all the appearance of having been constructed for the staging of theater. One wall of this intimate outdoor opera house is the facade of San Ignazio.

As one enters the church one's gaze is almost immediately drawn to the central ceiling panel, a *trompe-l'oeil* masterpiece completed in 1694 by the famed Jesuit artist Brother Andrea Pozzo, entitled "The Glory (or Apotheosis) of St. Ignatius." Pozzo, a master of perspective and foreshortening, succeeded not only in rendering three dimensions on a virtually flat surface, but in opening up the ceiling of the church to the virtual infinity of celestial height. As the viewer stands firmly planted on the marble floor of the church, the temple seems to explode upward toward the central figures of Christ and Ignatius, who appear to be ascending into the heavens. Surrounding Ignatius are angels, and some of the newly named saints of the Society, among them "Italians, Spaniards, Poles, French and Flemish . . . [who] symbolise St. Ignatius' international and supernational idea."[2]

Surrounding these international figures are clusters of groups representing struggling human beings in all their variety and difference, misery, confusion, and need. And these are not only European or Roman people; they comprise the palette of humanity from Europe to Asia, from Africa to the Americas — the entire expanding world toward which the young Society of Jesus was turning, especially through the ministry of the Roman College. In Pozzo's ceiling, God's saving light moves downward from the heavens toward all the peoples of the earth; the entire earth is suffused with the illumination of the heavens. At the same time, the viewer, along with the entire sweep of humanity, is drawn back up to that very focal point of heavenly glory toward which the ceiling is perpetually open. Pozzo has managed to depict a kind of back-and-forth movement of the religious imagination of the viewer, planted firmly on *terra firma,* but pointing upward toward the representation of earthly hope.

A yet closer look at the ceiling will demonstrate more clearly how this back-and-forth movement of the imagination functions. Although the geometrical focal point of light in the work is Ignatius, Ignatius is not placed dead center in the composition. That place is held by the glorified Jesus, who bears the cross upon his shoulder. He is gesturing toward Ignatius, beckoning him to his destiny, which is the destiny of the entire suffering world.[3]

Those familiar with the life of Ignatius will recognize here reference to the vision of Ignatius at La Storta, where Ignatius, upon entering Rome, had a life-changing vision of Jesus bearing his cross — a vision that resulted in a confirmation of his calling to Rome and in special reverence for the name of Jesus.[4] The movement between earth and heaven therefore finds its central mediation not in the final glory of Ignatius, but in the contemplation of the glory of God in the cross of Christ, who "'for a little while' was made 'lower than the angels,' that by the grace of God he might taste death for everyone" (Heb. 2:9).

Pozzo was not only a magnificently gifted artist; he was also a Jesuit. One can see in this ceiling the lines of the Ignatian religious imagination found in the Spiritual Exercises of St. Ignatius, the fundamental inspiration of the Jesuit approach to the Gospel.[5] Even the La Storta vision, which would seem to be a source for this fresco, must be read within the broader context of the Spiritual Exercises, where the main dynamics of Ignatian imagination are clearly indicated. For the Exercises chart a path that moves through the imagination between life on earth and an eschatological hope that is grounded in earthly life. Although the conclusion of the Exercises is called the "Contemplation to Attain Divine Love" (the "Contemplatio"), this end is attained within and not beyond the theater of the world of human actions, for it is only through this graced and struggling movement of human earthly life that one can adore the great saving work of God. Love for God in God's works of salvation is "precisely the object of Ignatian contemplation, of apostolic contemplation."[6] Ignatian contemplation calls for a full exercise of the religious imagination, finding in the real human world the struggle of God working out the liberation of the suffering people. The imagination for Ignatius is firmly planted in the human reality of space and time; it is within that reality — its temporality, spatiality, architecture, perspective, and motion — that God is experienced. And at the center of it, as in Pozzo's masterpiece, the cross is hovering, floating, as it were, between earth and heaven.

This centrality of the cross in Ignatian imagination gives rise to a theology of the cross in relation to suffering. A theology of the cross coming out of this tradition bears three distinctive marks: it reflects fully the reality of suffering that leads to death; it is related to the whole of the Paschal Mystery (from the incarnation to the resurrection); and it stands as a symbol of hope. The cross reveals a resurrection which is not only a future hope, but a reality occurring in history as people take others down from the crosses of suffering. As such, the cross is central to a Christian eschatology that not only points to a future, but draws human beings together in solidarity as they put themselves at the service of the promised hope which the resurrection reveals.

The Cross as Symbol of Suffering and Death

The cross is a steady imaginative symbol at work in the Exercises. At the end of the "First Week" or stage of the Exercises, Ignatius instructs that one kneel at the foot of the cross to contemplate where one stands in relation to Jesus — where one's life is going — and to pray for the poverty, humility, and humiliations that Jesus himself encountered.[7] And in the "Third Week," he suggests that we let our imaginations roam the full range of what Jesus himself experienced in his suffering and death, as well as what his companions, and in particular his mother, experienced.[8]

With the cross so central a fixture, how does the Christian escape despair, and find hope in the darkness of suffering and death? As we have seen, in the theology of Karl Rahner, it is a matter of grace, "the co-existential of pessimism" communicated by God to the human person.[9] But it also a matter of that person's active surrender to this grace, however darkly given, precisely by embracing what is awful and dreadful, much as did the father in Miller's parable of the gay son's suicide. For grace often enough comes in darkness, and it is the awful darkness that one sees, not what one expects the grace to be. How many people would immediately see God's grace arriving in the suffering of a loved one from AIDS or breast cancer, or would embrace these realities without dread? There is a seemingly natural tendency to pull back from darkness, to avoid the darkness and thus the grace that is, as it were, forced upon us by the trials of life.

For Rahner, however, the Christian posture toward reality is to face reality and try to acknowledge it as it is, not in a position of fatalism, but in an active surrender which is at the same time an acceptance of God's dark grace. Rahner here speaks of our knowingly "falling into the abyss of God's incomprehensibility."[10] At this point theology folds into its source, which is the experience of God as Mystery.

In Rahner's theology of death, this falling into the divine abyss in hope is the way in which Christians might approach their own death.[11] We can learn much about Christian hope, in fact, by thoroughly contemplating death, as Rahner urged. For Rahner, as for Heidegger, death is not limited to the physical demise and climax of organic human life. Rather, it is a permanent mark of the human situation. We are "beings-toward-death" from the moment of our conception. We are, in fact, from the moment of our birth, dying by installments throughout the time that binds our lives.[12]

Nevertheless, like the suffering that leads to it, death ordinarily comes to us against our wills. Death comes as an active force which we cannot escape. We must finally accept it and come to terms with our dying, with our very own death. Rahner suggests that Christians can, through an active faith, imagine dying as a gradual handing over of themselves to God with ever increasing desire and willingness. This is a matter of facing death head-on, a going through it. There is not only a passive dimension to death, in which death is imposed upon us, but also an active dimension, in which we dispossess ourselves and, with God's grace, let ourselves fall into the abyss of death willingly as the defining orientation of our lives.[13] For Rahner, an "active consummation" of life characterizes a precisely Christian death.[14] As the shifting boundaries of earthy life gradually dissolve through the organic processes of dying, so, too, can this active surrendering bring us to the point of expressing a profound "yes" to God with our lives. The moments of dying are not limited strictly to the deathbed itself or to the final breath. That particular temporal occasion is only the emphatic end of a reality that stretches over a lifetime, and comes into dramatic focus in the sufferings of a life that culminates inevitably in death.

Here the cross enters the picture. It is not accidental but essential to Christian self-understanding that the cross should stand as the central symbol of faith. The cross reminds us of the stark reality of the human condition, its entwinement in the sin of the world, and its inherent ambiguity as the locus of human guilt and divine mercy. The cross not only reminds us of the harsh and dark realities of life, but also that we cannot evade them in the name of religion, or for that matter, in the name of compassion. Quite the opposite, in fact. For the cross says that death is not simply a part of the future, but, as Simone Weil rightly put it in another context, death *is* the future.[15]

> Those who remember that even the incarnate God Himself could not look on the rigours of destiny without anguish, should understand that men can only appear to elevate themselves above human misery by disguising the rigours of destiny in their own eyes, by the help of illusion, of intoxication, or of fanaticism. Unless protected by an armour of lies, man cannot endure might without suffering a blow in the depth of his soul. Grace can prevent this blow from corrupting the soul, but cannot prevent its wound.[16]

Rahner wrote stirringly that "Christianity is the religion which recognizes a man who was nailed to a cross and on it died a violent death *as a sign of victory* and as a realistic expression of human life."[17] Thus, it is properly the central symbol of Christian faith. On the cross Jesus finally surrenders himself to the abyss of darkness threatened by creaturely nothingness. His falling into the void of death was at the same time a release into the mystery of God. This release is the graced destiny of all, though one made terrifying by the involvement of guilt in our physical demise. The cross of Jesus is therefore a symbol of the intrinsic connection between the sin of the world and death, even as it also stands as the threshold of hope.[18] This is why the cross is such an important symbol in Christian self-understanding, because on it the sorrow of suffering was fully embraced by God in Jesus and hope was mysteriously born. Death, even the darkest, is not merely the necessary experience of submission to an inevitable clinical demise. From a theological point of view, precisely as a dying, it can also be seen and perhaps even entered into by some as an active surrender to the God of hope.[19]

One arrives finally at a stance within existence that is anchored in, redeemed by hope: a surrender of everything through dying to God, even from the earliest stirrings of a human life. For a Christian "... believes that everything positive and beautiful and everything which blossoms has to pass through what we call death."[20] This stance is consistent with a quiet joy in life and a love for life that in no way denies the bleak landscapes of human existence but opens life to the future of God. As Rahner observed:

> We come from a beginning we did not choose and go to an end that is lost in God.... We never know with ultimate certitude how we relate with our freedom to the inescapable situation of our existence; we have to accept our beginning, give our ultimate love to the end we call God, and with hope leave whether or not we do it in God's hands.[21]

Dying understood as ongoing active surrender to God is consistent with the turn toward the eschatological horizon of hope against which the cross stands.

The Cross in Relation to the Whole Paschal Mystery

Some might say that Rahner's theology of death runs the risk here of setting up a romanticized view of death, some ideal death that becomes one more item on the checklist of Christian perfectionism. Even the lives of the saints attest that there is no perfect death. Particularly instructive was the death of Thérèse from the horrible pains of tuberculosis. This was no passive passage into the realm of light and bliss. The Saint found herself in the throes of a massive spiritual struggle, an entanglement with deepest darkness.[22] Often enough death from other dread diseases, such as AIDS, hardly allows for the kind of active surrender that Rahner is talking about, at least at the very moment of death itself. If dying involves an active surrender to God's darkly given grace, this runs so deeply against human instinct that it must depend on something more than human beings can muster on their own. It must also depend on God's own gracious participation.

In the Ignatian imagination, that participation is ongoing. God started participating in the sufferings of the human lot in the incarnation itself. In the Spiritual Exercises, the conclusion of the final "Contemplatio," a sense of God's love descending from above and working on our behalf and participating in our lives, cannot be attained apart from the pivotal contemplation on the incarnation. Mindfulness of the cross begins with the meditation on the incarnation, which will lead to the cross and culminate in the revelation of God's saving work in the resurrection.

The contemplation on the incarnation is situated within the "Second Week" of the Spiritual Exercises, a phase during which the pilgrim (the person undertaking the Exercises as a spiritual practice, and a name Ignatius gave to himself), having already savored the consolation of knowing that one is a sinner loved by God, is now freed to focus on his or her desire for and generosity for serving God in one's life. The pilgrim has already undertaken the "Kingdom" contemplation, in which one is asked to consider Jesus' invitation: "Whoever would like to come with me is to labor with me that following me in the pain, that person may also follow me in the glory."[23] She was further invited to consider the following type of prayer of self-offering, where, with the help of God's infinite goodness, one expresses the "want and desire and deliberate determination...to imitate you in bearing all injuries and abuse and all poverty of spirit, and actual poverty, too, if your most Holy Majesty wants to choose and receive me to such life and state."[24] This is a prayer for the grace to enter into the reality of human life as it is, into the world of suffering, and of hope.

The contemplation itself consists of a brief preparatory prayer, three preludes, three points, and one so-called colloquy.

The first prelude begins with a colloquy among the three divine persons in the heavens, perhaps like the divine cluster at the center of Pozzo's ceiling. As Ignatius frames it:

> Here, it is how the three divine persons looked at all the plain or circuit of all the world, full of people, and how, seeing that all

were going down to hell, it is determined in their eternity, that
the second person should become human to save the human
race. . . . [25]

The initiative of a movement between earth and heaven begins entirely with God, *de arriba*, in the interest of saving a lost
human race.

The second prelude shifts the focus from the Trinity to that singular, unique human person, Mary of Nazareth, to whom the Trinity
has chosen to communicate itself. Mary is seen "within the great
capacity and circuit of the world, in which are so many and such different people."[26] Here, the gaze of the imagination is drawn toward
the richly variegated human world in which we are planted, depicted
in Pozzo's fresco by so many different types of people, and, ultimately,
to a consideration of the particularity of each person.

The third prelude is an exercise in drawing the first two together
through an "interior knowledge" of Jesus, "Who for me has been made
human, that I may more love and follow him."[27] The economy of
heaven and earth, the divine action made on behalf of all humanity,
is also made "for me" with the end in mind that I might live for God's
purposes. The Mediator, Jesus, is therefore "at once in heaven and
here below." The pilgrim's focus upon Jesus draws the imagination
up into the mystery of God, but without losing earthly traction.

Ignatius invites the pilgrim to experience this movement of the
imagination, and to retain a sense of life as it is, by focusing on
the bodily senses. The bodily senses become an integral part of the
function of the religious imagination — an imagination exercised not
in abstraction from, but precisely through, the human body: "seeing"
and "hearing" "first those [persons] on the surface of the earth, in
such diversity, in dress as in actions: some white and others black;
some in peace and others in war; some weeping and others laughing;
some well, others ill; some being born and others dying, etc."[28]

All of this leads to an understanding of the context within which
the incarnation takes place, and to a sensory meditation on the
nativity itself, beginning with Mary's *fiat* in Nazareth, and becoming
real in the Bethlehem stable.

Rahner reminds us, however, that the crib at Bethlehem points inevitably through the darkness of suffering that is to reach its climax on the cross. The meaning of the cross as a path to hope is anchored not only in the agonies of Jesus' own passion, but even in the promise of his life at his birth as a human being. It includes the whole of the Paschal Mystery. "We should notice here," Rahner wrote, "that He came into the world the same way we did in order to come to terms with the pre-given facts of human existence, and to begin to die as we all do."[29] As birth is tied to death, so is the incarnation intrinsically tied to the destiny of Jesus on the cross. Rahner expressed this linkage between birth, death, and final hope in a poignant Christmas meditation which focuses, ironically, on newborn life: "When we stand in faith before the Child's crib, we have to see that it is here that the decline called death begins, that descent which alone saves because its emptiness is filled with unutterable inconceivability of God. . . . "[30]

The Cross as Revelation of Hope

Hope is a name for the orientation of human beings toward the God who is not only the source and sustainer of all that is, but who is the one who anoints this existence with the divine self-gift. God promises to be "my good," "our good." The horizon of hope is thus the personal God who is the beginning and end of human existence, and who encompasses all human existence in a personally bestowed providence. Hope, however, is not merely a matter of deciding to turn ourselves over, through some heroic and possibly hubristic spiritual act, to the infinite context of our lives, and thus to be spared the real pains and sorrows of this earthly existence. For although hope is, in a transcendental sense, the goal of our spiritual freedom, we only know it precisely within the real, within experiences of suffering. As Rahner saw, we gain a deeper sense of hope as we see earthly realities more and more as provisional, passing, and incomprehensible.[31] Hope as a theological virtue, a habitual bearing toward God given by God and revealing of God, becomes a reality in direct proportion to our acceptance of the ultimate incomprehensibility of existence.[32]

Thus, the Christian cannot deny the sting of suffering and death in the name of hope. As Paul reminds us, Christians are baptized into hope because they are baptized into Christ's death (Rom. 6:3). Reality pushes toward the truth of its brutal end. A facile optimism about life and what we can accomplish within it "is excluded by the Christian conviction that we arrive at God's definitive realm only by passing through death...."[33] All of life's perplexity is finally confronted by the perplexity of death itself, that "radical fall into the abyss of divinity" which is "the experience of the arrival of God."[34]

The catch, as I noted in chapter 1, is that the promises we hope for are never fully realized within the space of human life. This can lead to a profound sense of futility, even hopelessness and despair. Here, too, the cross is pivotal, for on it the Son of God himself experienced what it means to be on the precipice of hopelessness, of sinking into an unfathomable darkness. And people of faith know this kind of cross. Rahner says, "we suffer because *God* seems to be far from us." But the emphasis here is on *God*, for what Rahner wishes to suggest is that when this is the case, we may well be assuming a god who is not the God of radical involvement in human life by virtue of the incarnation itself. If we can see the cross of human existence in light of God's present and radical involvement in human life itself, then we need not fear even despair:

Indeed, we can truly say: in this experience of the heart, let yourself seemingly accept with calm every despair. Let despair fill your heart so that there no longer seems to remain an exit to life, to fulfillment, to space and to God. In despair, despair not. Let yourself accept everything; in reality it is only an acceptance of the finite and the futile.... Do not be frightened over the loneliness and abandonment of your interior dungeon, which seems to be so dead — like a grave. For if you stand firm, if you do not run from despair, if in despair over the idols which up to now you called God you do not despair in the true God, if you thus stand firm — this is already a wonder of grace — then you will suddenly perceive that your grave-dungeon only blocks the futile finiteness; you will become aware that your deadly void is only the breadth of God's intimacy, that the silence is filled up by a word without words, by the one who is above all names and is all in all.... Notice that God is there.[35]

For Rahner, as for Ignatius, the cross, in its stark reality, is the revelation of the abiding presence of the God who is always radically present to and within human experience, even if He cannot be detected. It is true that Ignatius urges that one seek the God who "hides itself" in the real sufferings of Jesus on the cross and how this divinity seemingly "leaves the most sacred humanity to suffer so very cruelly."[36] Yet, the cross in one sense finally has nothing to do with this God, a God who is absent. The God of Jesus hardly wants this suffering to befall him. Jesus' suffering and death, which make no human sense, and are experiences of utter absurdity on the human side of the scale, nevertheless occur within the ambit of a God whose love is both silent and close.

An Ignatian Eschatology: Living the Resurrection

As I have already stated, the motion of the Ignatian imagination is a hopeful one, reaching toward a transcendent vision, the risen life, but firmly rooted in the harsh realities of the world, where God entered as a suffering human being. It is a hope that we begin to see realized in activity in the world. Ignacio Ellacuría, the slain Rector of the Jesuit University of Central America in El Salvador, called it living "as already risen beings."[37] This sense of living in hope, "doing" resurrection, goes all the way back to Ignatius of Loyola himself. Early Jesuits like Jerónimo Nadal "affirmed straightforwardly that for the members of the order 'the world' was their 'house' [and]... that the Society was essentially a group 'on mission,' ready at any moment to travel to any point where there was need for its ministry." The doing of the saving work of the Gospel anywhere in the world is firmly planted in the heart of the Jesuit imagination.[38] This imagination leads from earth to heaven in the human desire for God; at the same time, it leads from heaven to earth in God's desire, working through the willing cooperation of human beings, for the liberation of human beings. Philip Endean notes: "In Ignatian imaginative prayer, we are invited to experiment with new ways of understanding the world.... We seek to let the Gospel symbols be reflected in our own selves, generating new patterns of interpretation and action.... An awareness of dependence on God enables and expands us to be who we are. Our ultimate categories are relational."[39]

Jon Sobrino, one of the chief architects of the theology of liberation, has noted the frequent and historic gap between spirituality as theory and spirituality as the practice of Christian faith, a gap which the theology of liberation has endeavored to bridge.[40] The spiritual life, he reminds us, is never purely spiritual; it must include real "incarnated" life, the edges of history as people experience and construct history. It is in this historical theater of human experience that the Paschal Mystery has taken place, not outside of it. As the martyrdom of his brother Jesuits in 1989 attested, such a conviction is bound to bring with it a certain definite rejection and persecution, responses that would not exist if real life were not the basis for a spiritual vision.[41] Spiritual life, therefore, is planted "from below," from the standpoint of the one "looking up" to the God who liberates human beings from the structures of sin which pull them down.

At the same time, it must be said that historical life is never purely a matter of the concrete and material.[42] This is a fundamental insight of the Hegelian dialectic of history, which sees history as the unfurling of the Spirit through human contingencies. In Jesus himself, it is not merely his own initiative, but the initiative of the Spirit which impels him, through his freedom, toward undertaking a ministry of salvation, indeed of liberating the lowliest from their oppression. The ultimate impetus for the saving work of Christ comes "from above" as the triune God chooses to become one with humanity in the form of a slave, a suffering servant.

Sobrino specifies four prerequisites for an understanding of the cross in relation to the resurrection, an understanding deeply imbued with the Ignatian imagination. The first is "honesty to the real," which means beginning with the human condition as it is.[43] Sobrino begins with a firm stance in the world of the suffering poor, those who have been systematically excised from pictures of what is "real." This is a major and repeated theme in Ignatian spirituality, where Ignatius suggests that the pilgrim pray for the grace of joining Jesus in his poverty, even if this means actual poverty. This is remarkably represented in the Pozzo ceiling, with teeming masses of poor humanity of all colors reaching up to heaven for salvation. The viewer stands spatially within the world of this teeming poor humanity, not above them, nor to the side, merely looking on. The aesthetic and spiritual effect is one of radical involvement within their worlds, even identification with "those on the lowest rung of the ladder of history."[44]

The second prerequisite is "fidelity to the real," which Sobrino describes as perseverance in our original honesty, however we may be burdened with, even engulfed in, the negative elements of history. Our first knowing of the harsh truths of life is daunting, and the sheer power of negativity will challenge any hope we might bring to reality. Yet, as we have seen in this book, we must face reality, all of it. We shall know only that we must stay faithful, keep moving ahead in history, striving ever to transform that history from negative to positive.[45] Again, we find ourselves planted so firmly in the "below" of history that the vision of an integral liberation can be clouded. Looking "up" we can, perhaps, fail to see, or want to circumvent the fact, that a central mediation of the liberating work of the Gospel is the suffering of the cross born by the one who becomes incarnate within human history. Fidelity to the real reveals that liberation is not a matter of theory alone, but of the interplay between flesh and spirit, and therefore, of suffering and hope, perhaps leading even to martyrdom.[46] Fidelity to the real, furthermore, has a practical dimension that is integral to it. This means actively participating in the work of liberation, *doing* it. In Pozzo's ceiling, the triune God establishes the pattern for active participation: full incarnation by entering centrally into the drama of the human condition in its poorest and most abject form.

This leads to the third prerequisite of a spirituality of the cross: the willingness to be swept along by the "more" of reality.[47] Here Sobrino strikes a familiar Ignatian theme, the idea of the *magis* or the *more*. The *magis* is a way of speaking of an active openness to the totality of human reality, and the willingness to be caught up in it. But the Ignatian imagination, while firmly planted in human reality, decenters the world of the familiar, the world that is given, and turns one's attention to the world as God sees it, as we noted in the Ignatian contemplation on the incarnation. We have seen how this divine view can be understood as the divine empathy for those who suffer. This means that the world is always a bigger place than we can see from any one perspective, and the theater of suffering, too, is larger and more daunting than our own personal sufferings can allow us to capture. So we must look beyond ourselves and our own sufferings to the whole theater of human suffering, and enter into that wider world. For it is the whole world of suffering that is met by the divine empathy in the incarnation that leads to the cross.

Fourth, the divine empathy is mediated in and through human empathy, solidarity among the sufferers. In Pozzo's ceiling, Europe, the only world familiar to most seventeenth-century viewers, is put in perspective and even reduced in status to one of the four corners of the earth, on a par with the Americas, Asia, and Africa. At the same time, it finds a new sense of itself as a culture among cultures, where human misery and poverty are shared transculturally, as much in need of the liberating work of the incarnation as is Africa, Asia, or the Americas. While in each of these mythic places, the Gospel becomes allegorized according to native custom and costume, a new center now holds, not in the culture of Europe, but in the liberating work of God, coalesced in the cross which hovers at the center. And here, Sobrino gives us a beautiful image of what it means to live the resurrection, to do the work of the resurrection, to live in service of it: People of faith in the resurrection show that faith by helping those who suffer, letting them down from their crosses. If the resurrection is the reversal of the cross, it means the end to the sufferings of the cross, and the beginning of new life, a release from those sufferings. This is the *eschatological* hope of Christian faith: final freedom from suffering, the wounds of human suffering met by the kiss of God. But this eschatological hope is realized, gradually, in the present times of history, as human beings enter into solidarity with one another, take one another down from their crosses. It is a hope planted in the real, ever in the process of being realized, and only fulfilled in the final (as yet hidden) reality of God.

It is here that Sobrino points to the essential prerequisite of the experience of God.[48] There is no spiritual experience that is not framed by history. In the movement of Ignatian imagination, that experience is the experience of salvation, of a total and integral liberation of human beings from suffering. The saving work of God is an ongoing labor of God himself which takes place within the theater of human suffering, especially the suffering of the poor and afflicted, into whose particular world the incarnate One entered. In the last analysis we are speaking here of a spirituality which is most accessible not only in the texts of various editions of the Exercises, nor in the visual splendor of great church ceilings, but primarily in the fabric of human lives, which Ignatius in his genius saw as yearning for salvation. This spiritual path through the motion of the religious imagination is of particular pertinence in our own day, when the earthly and transcendent poles are often enough proposed as mutually exclusive opposites, and where God, who seems distant from human life and our suffering, is reserved to the realm of private judgment, or worse, to flights of religious escapism. A Christian imagination thoroughly grounded in concrete human experience, as this one surely is, can only conclude to a God who is correlatively real and liberating.

The Ignatian imagination approaches the cross as a sign of hope for all of those who suffer. For in that Ignatian imagination, eschatology is not an otherworldly dream; it is the revelation of God that occurs within human life as it is, within the theater of life's dark suffering. The cross looms as a symbol of the earthly sojourn that we know only too well, but also, in Jesus, as the total entrance of God, from the point of the incarnation, into that world of suffering. And, just as Jesus was raised from the dead, herein lies the hope that life, God's life, will finally prevail, and that those who are suffering are already being raised.

Afterword

The Cross as Path to Joy

Miracle! Look, Father, look: the spots have disappeared from my skin! I am healed!
— Olivier Messiaen, *Saint François d'Assise*
Troisième Tableau, Kissing the Leper

OLIVIER MESSIAEN'S OPERA *Saint François d'Assise* is a miraculous expression of Christian faith, the center of which is the cross with which Francis so totally identified that he suffered the stigmata. But the cross in this opera is also the path to joy; it is by going through it that Francis is freed from his own fears, freed in order to love. The leper, in turn, is freed from the cross of his own suffering, and, when Francis kisses his wounds, the leper dances with joy. The crucible of suffering has become the chalice of reconciliation and love. In the final act, on Francis's deathbed, the leper returns to welcome him into the joys of heaven, where he will be able to listen forever to the music of the Invisible. Here is an image of the hope that Christian faith says our sufferings may reveal.

This book is the fruit of reflections undertaken during the past ten years, during which time I have searched for a similar image of hope. The search was precipitated by the long illnesses and eventual deaths of my sister and brother, one from breast cancer and the other from HIV/AIDS. They finally died within nine months of each other. Both of them died on crosses of incomprehensible suffering, suffering that enveloped every dimension of their lives. Accompanying them to their deaths forced me to reflect not only upon the mystery of suffering in everyday life, but the reach of suffering in both its spiritual depths and its wider, even historic scales. This book is dedicated to the memory and inspiration of my sister and brother. What happened over ten years ago is the driving force behind my writing it.

For my sister and brother, the reality of death's blow was compounded by their relative youth, and by the fact that both had led lives of some pain and suffering that somehow came to expression in the untimeliness and cruelty of the modes of their dying.

David's dying was bound up with the difficulties of trying to work out his homosexuality in cultural and ecclesiastical environments that did not foster self-acceptance, much less the living out of integral, balanced relationships between homosexual people. In David's life, as in the lives of so many other deeply closeted young gay men growing up in the 1970s, a fully integrated and open life as a gay man remained a thwarted dream. My sister Sheila had also suffered much, and in great silence. Behind the bouncy smile there was a mystery to her life that I will never be able to unravel. The common element of their lives, a great interior suffering, entered into their physical suffering as well. It was a suffering that was brought to an end only in their deaths.

And then there was my mother, already in her mid-seventies. (My father had died ten years earlier.) Her felt loss was beyond my reckoning. At David's funeral she spoke to everyone assembled through one of Rilke's poems:

> Now my anguish is complete. It is unspeakable,
> it fills me. I am numb
> like the stone's core.
> I am hard, and know only one thing:
> you grew big —
> ... and grew big,
> in order to stand outside
> my heart, an agony
> bigger than it is capable of.
> Now you're lying right across my lap,
> now I can no longer give you
> birth.[1]

My mother's grief only compounded my own sense of incomprehen-sion over the loss of my sister and brother. And so their suffering and deaths have haunted me, and left me asking questions, looking for answers.

Perhaps it might seem odd to say it, but in the aftermath of their deaths, I was not "angry" with God. I was instead left numb and speechless. Recognition of anger of a far deeper kind, accompanied by the depression it engendered, was to come later, when, perhaps like Sölle's worker, I was yearning for a scream that would not come forth. Instead, I managed to see what had happened as well within the statistical range of probability, or the sheer randomness of human events. Furthermore, I asked, why should any of us be exempt from suffering, even from what we might consider to be improbable suf-fering? And, of course, I knew then that there are people who have suffered far greater losses, or who were even then suffering chronically and tragically far beyond my own imaginings. For we can encounter these forms of suffering on a steady basis, if not in our own lives, then surely in the lives of others and in the daily news.

But these rationalizations were, of course, attempts to avoid what I had to face, much as the father in Miller's parable initially searched for ways around having to delve into the truth of the tragedy that had beset him.

And so I began to wonder about the deeper questions, however predictable and ordinary they might have seemed: Does the suffering that attends life in fact have any meaning, or is life itself simply a string of meaningless happenings, a final absurdity? And where is God in all of this? Present? Absent? Wringing his hands? Does God even care? And, perhaps the most persistent question for me: Why the Cross? Not only what is the meaning of all this suffering that besets the human race, but why does this suffering, symbolized by the Cross, apparently lie at the heart of the Christian faith and its imagination? How can one possibly hope for a better future, or a future in a loving God, in the face of so much darkness — suffering compounding suffering, an endless chronicle of it? What would it mean to hope, to believe in a resurrection from the dead — a triumph over and release from all of this?

What became apparent to me was that the suffering and deaths of my sister and brother constituted a life-transforming event for them, for me, as well as for my mother. I was at a crossroads, where I could attempt a retreat into an older and familiar world, or where I would have to face squarely what these events were calling me to face. I realized that I could only begin to glean some answers to my questions, questions that sprang from so much anguish, if I faced all the suffering squarely, and went where it would lead me, even if I did not want to go there.

There are times when the suffering that attends tragic reversal, both in one's own life or in the lives of others, forces upon us a wisdom that is not asked for, not even wanted. But that very wisdom can become a key to a joyful freedom, where one discovers all of a sudden, as if awakened from a long trance, that what once seemed very important simply no longer has any power over us. What ultimately matters, instead, is the joy that one discovers, as Francis did, when he kissed the leper, and the joy the leper discovered when, against all earthly hope, he was finally set free. In Messiaen's opera, the leper springs into a wondrous dance of joy. In the final analysis, we are, each and all of us, lepers — waiting to be kissed, yearning to dance with joy. God's accomplishment of this in us, entering into and working through our sorrows and sufferings, is the gift of what Ignatius called the "Contemplatio," the hope of faith fulfilled, not by us, but by God. Precisely by living in and going through our sufferings, we can in fact enter into joy — perhaps a quiet joy, but nevertheless real. The final hope of Christian faith is that this reality, the reality of joy born of suffering, may become good news for all the suffering world.

Notes

Preface

1. Aeschylus, *Oresteia,* trans. Richmond Lattimore (Chicago: University of Chicago Press, 1953), 40. Cf. translation of Paul Roche, *The Orestes Plays of Aeschylus* (New York: Mentor Books, 1962), 37:

> He leads us on the way of wisdom's
> Everlasting law that truth
> Is only learnt by suffering it.
> Ah, in sleep the pain distills,
> Bleeding on the memory,
> And makes us wise against our wills:
> God's grace by solemn force.

2. Jerome Miller, *The Way of Suffering, A Geography of Crisis* (Washington, DC: Georgetown University Press, 1988), 5.

3. Thomas Aquinas argues that hope is "theological" in that God is the principal object or final end of this virtue, and also its efficient cause: "... quod quaecumque alia spes adipisci expectat, sperat in ordine ad Deum sicut ad ultimum finem et sicut ad primam causam efficientem...." In other words, the virtue has its origin in God's self-gift of grace, and finds its fulfillment in God himself. *Summa Theologiae,* II-II, q.15 ad 1, in Biblioteca de Autores Cristianos (Madrid, 1952), 3: 116.

4. Dennis Marshall, "Into the Inescapable Darkness: Karl Rahner's Theology of Redemptive Suffering," diss. (Duquesne University, 1997). See especially his treatment of the critiques of Johannes Metz, Elizabeth Johnson, Hans Urs von Balthasar, and Walter Kasper, 1–45.

5. See ibid., n. 187, for an extensive listing of works that treat of suffering in its many and various forms, where Marshall lists twenty-five articles from the *Theological Investigations* alone. Yet, even this impressive list is significantly incomplete.

6. See Michael Barnes, "Demythologization in the Theology of Karl Rahner," *Theological Studies* 55 (1994): 24–45.

7. Hans Urs von Balthasar, *The Moment of Christian Witness,* trans. Richard Beckley (Glen Rock, NJ: Newman, 1966), 64.

8. On the notion of *existentiell*, see Karl Rahner, *Foundations of Christian Faith: An Introduction to the Idea of Christianity*, trans. William V. Dych (New York: Crossroad, 1978), 305–7.

Chapter 1: The Terrain of Suffering

1. David Tracy, "Evil, Suffering, Hope: The Search for New Forms of Contemporary Theodicy," *Proceedings of the Catholic Theological Society of America* 50 (1995): 16.

2. See Johannes Metz, "The Church after Auschwitz," in *A Passion for God: The Mystical-Political Dimension of Christianity*, trans. J. Matthew Ashley (New York: Paulist, 1998), 121–32.

3. Roger Haight, *Jesus: Symbol of God* (Maryknoll, NY: Orbis, 1999), 25.

4. Edward Schillebeeckx, *Christ: The Experience of Jesus as Lord*, trans. John Bowden (New York: Crossroad, 1989), 729.

5. For more on AIDS understood as plague, see Susan Sontag, *Illness as Metaphor and AIDS and Its Metaphors* (New York: Doubleday, 1990), and for an alternative view, see Andrew Sullivan, "When Plagues End: A Reflection on the Passing of a Crisis," *New York Times Magazine*, November 10, 1996, 52ff.

6. Schillebeeckx, *Christ*, 725.

7. Jon Sobrino, *Where Is God? Earthquake, Terrorism, Barbarity, and Hope* (Maryknoll, NY: Orbis, 2004), 112.

8. *The Complete Edition of the Oxford English Dictionary* (1971), II:3141.

9. Rahner, *Encounters with Silence*, trans. James M. Demske (Westminster, MD: Newman Press, 1960), 54.

10. Bernard of Clairvaux, Sermon 26, *The Works of Bernard of Clairvaux*, vol. 3, trans. Kilian Walsh (Kalamazoo, MI: Cistercian Publications, 1976), 60–61.

11. C. S. Lewis, *A Grief Observed* (London: Faber and Faber, 1961), 7.

12. Experience is a notoriously difficult term to control. It also runs the risk of defying any mapping at all because of the rhetorical appeal to one's "own experience," something that cannot be gainsaid. For a discussion of this problem, see George Schner, "The Appeal to Experience," *Theological Studies* 53 (1992): 40–59. In general, "experience" presumes three terms: an objective reality that meets or acts upon a person (subject), a subject thus acted upon, and an interpretation of the encounter undertaken by the subject in relation to other subjects and actors.

13. But, as Simone Weil notes, "An hour or two of violent pain caused by a decayed tooth is nothing once it is over." "The Love of God and Affliction," in *Waiting for God*, trans. Emma Craufurd (New York: Harper and Row, 1951), 118.

14. Sontag, *Illness as Metaphor and AIDS and Its Metaphors* (New York: Doubleday Anchor, 1990), 23.

15. Ibid., 102.

16. William Lynch, *Images of Hope: Imagination as Healer of the Hopeless* (Notre Dame: University of Notre Dame Press, 1965), 25.

17. Ibid.

18. Hans Georg Gadamer, *The Enigma of Health: The Art of Healing in a Scientific Age*, trans. Jason Gaiger and Nicholas Walker (Stanford: Stanford University Press, 1996), 111. For the destructive perceptions of diseased persons by the well, especially perceptions of the mentally ill and those suffering from sexually transmitted diseases, including AIDS, see Sander L. Gilman, *Disease and Representation: Images of Illness from Madness to AIDS* (Ithaca, NY: Cornell University Press, 1988).

19. Weil, "The Love of God and Affliction," 117–19.

20. Weil, "Spiritual Autobiography," in *Waiting for God*, 68. Simone Pétrement makes much of Weil's headaches, reporting that the pain was so intense that at one point she considered suicide. See *Simone Weil: A Life*, trans. Raymond Rosenthal (New York: Pantheon, 1976), 339.

21. Weil, "The Love of God and Affliction," 117–18.

22. Ibid., 120.

23. Ibid., 117–18.

24. Ibid., 119.

25. Ibid.

26. Ibid., 120.

27. Ibid., 119–20.

28. Ibid., 120, 122.

29. Ibid., 121, 122.

30. Ibid., 123.

31. Ibid., 124. For more on the agony of suffering psychic pain in the midst of a world of the unafflicted, see Kay Redfield Jamison in *An Unquiet Mind: A Memoir of Moods and Madness* (New York: Vintage, 1996); William Styron, *Darkness Visible: A Memoir of Madness* (New York: Random House, 1990); and Patrick J. Howell, SJ, *Reducing the Storm to a Whisper: The Story of a Breakdown* (Chicago: Thomas More, 1985). For an account of the search for hope through depression, see Jeffery Smith, *Where the Roots Reach for Water: A Personal and Natural History of Melancholia* (New York: North Point Press, 1999).

32. Tracy, "Evil, Suffering and Hope," 15.

33. This point is made, of course, by Kant in his *Religion within the Limits of Reason Alone*, trans. Theodore M. Greene and Hoyt H. Hudson (New York: Harper Torchbooks, 1960). For a contemporary illustration of the moral etiology of social evils, see Jonathan Glover, *Humanity: A Moral History of the Twentieth Century* (New Haven: Yale University Press, 1999). Among many examples, Glover treats of Nazism, Hiroshima, Stalinism, My Lai, and Rwanda.

34. Marilyn McCord Adams, *Horrendous Evils and the Goodness of God* (Ithaca, NY: Cornell University Press, 1999), 26.

35. Ibid., 26–27.

36. Elaine Scarry, *The Body in Pain: The Making and Unmaking of the World* (New York: Oxford University Press, 1985), 45.

37. Lynch, *Images of Hope*, 48–50.

38. Ibid., 56.

39. Ibid., 55.

40. Ibid., 55–56.
41. Ibid., 67–68.
42. Ibid., 72.
43. Ibid., 76.

Chapter 2: Facing the Reality of Suffering

1. Miller, *The Way of Suffering*, 49.

2. Pantxika Berguerie, *The Unterlinden Museum* (Colmar, France: Unterlinden Museum, 1999), 59.

3. His published works, especially those from the 1950s and early 1960s, give testimony to his interest in the intersection between Christian imagination and the arts: *The Image Industries* (New York: Sheed and Ward, 1959), *Christ and Apollo: The Dimensions of the Literary Imagination* (Notre Dame: University of Notre Dame Press, 1960), and *The Integrating Mind: An Exploration into Western Thought* (New York: Sheed and Ward, 1962). Later, in the 1970s, he was to produce two more works, *Christ and Prometheus: A New Image of the Secular* (Notre Dame: University of Notre Dame Press, 1970), and *Images of Faith: An Exploration into the Ironic Imagination* (Notre Dame: University of Notre Dame Press, 1973). For more information on Lynch's life, see Gerald J. Bednar, *Faith as Imagination: the Contribution of William F. Lynch, SJ* (Kansas City, MO: Sheed and Ward, 1996), xi–xiv.

4. They are, in order: "Theology and the Imagination," *Thought* 29 (1954): 61–86 [hereafter referenced as "Theology and Imagination I"]; "Theology and the Imagination II: The Evocative Symbol," *Thought* 29 (1954): 529–54 [hereafter referenced as "Theology and Imagination II"]; and "Theology and the Imagination III: The Problem of Comedy," *Thought* 30 (1955): 18–36 [hereafter referenced as "Theology and Imagination III"].

5. Lynch, "Theology and the Imagination I," 71.

6. Lynch, *Images of Hope*, 149.

7. Lynch, "Theology and the Imagination II," 546–47.

8. Ibid., 547. Bednar terms this a "metaphysics of interpenetration" (44–45).

9. Lynch, "Theology and the Imagination I," 75.

10. Ibid., 77.

11. Ibid., 79–82.

12. Lynch, "Theology and the Imagination III," 33. To my knowledge, this usage of the term antedates David Tracy's magisterial development of the term in *The Analogical Imagination* (New York: Crossroad, 1981).

13. For a thorough treatment of the analogical imagination according to Lynch, see Bednar, *Faith as Imagination*, 57–68.

14. Lynch's treatment of tragedy might well be read alongside other philosophical, religious, and theological treatments of it. For a classic philosophical exploration of the tragic as a spiritual sensibility, see Miguel de Unamuno, *The Tragic Sense of Life* (London: Collins, 1921; 1962). For a further philosophical development involving the thought of the Catholic existentialist Gabriel Marcel

and the phenomenologist Paul Ricoeur, see Gabriel Marcel, *Tragic Wisdom and Beyond* (Evanston: Northwestern University Press, 1973). For a scholarly investigation of tragedy as presented within the Bible, see J. Cheryl Exum, *Tragedy and Biblical Narrative* (Cambridge: Cambridge University Press, 1992.

15. For more on the relationship between tragedy and comedy in literature and drama, see Richard B. Sewall, *The Vision of Tragedy* (New Haven: Yale University Press, 1959), 1–2, and also 148 n. 1: "...tragedy cannot tell 'the whole truth.' The problem of the reader of tragedy is to be sensitive to the delicate interactions of the modes; and so he must understand comedy, too." The notion of a "tragic vision" of life, more psychological than literary, is developed by Murray Krieger in *The Tragic Vision: Variations on a Theme in Literary Imagination* (Chicago: University of Chicago Press, 1960).

16. Lynch, "Theology and the Imagination III," 24.

17. Ibid., 33. Lynch adds that, in contrast to the univocal mind, comedy "seems anarchic (and indeed it does have a propensity for thieves, villains, drunkards, fools, idiots, lawbreakers and other people like the reader and the writer)." (34)

18. Lynch, "Theology and the Imagination I," 65.

19. Lynch, "The Imagination of the Drama," *Review of Existential Psychology and Psychiatry* 14 (1975–76): 5–6.

20. Lynch, "Theology and the Imagination I," 67.

21. Ibid., 68.

22. Lynch, "Theology and the Imagination III," 18.

23. Lynch, "Theology and the Imagination II," 532.

24. Ibid., 530.

25. Ibid., 529–31.

26. But note how a clash ensued between the cross and the swastika with the advent of the Führer principle and the Aryan clause within the German Evangelical church. See Eberhard Bethge, *Dietrich Bonhoeffer: A Biography,* rev. ed. (Minneapolis: Fortress Press, 2000), 270–93.

27. For more on Lynch's breakdown, see Bednar, *Faith as Imagination,* xiii.

28. For a survey of the gradual and ambiguous embrace of psychological sciences by American Catholicism, see C. Kevin Gillespie, *Psychology and American Catholicism: From Confession to Therapy?* (New York: Crossroad, 2001).

29. Lynch, *Images of Hope,* 14.

30. Ibid., 21.

31. This is a thematic developed by Miller in *The Way of Suffering:* "Events no longer seem to affect him. He appears, in fact to have 'no affect,' as psychologists would say — to have lost his capacity for being emotionally engaged in the ebb and flow of daily existence. He seems 'dead.'" (67)

32. Lynch, *Images of Hope,* 36.

33. Ibid., 32.

34. Ibid., 33.

35. Ibid., 35.

36. Ibid., 36.

37. Ibid., 37.
38. Ibid., 48–50.
39. Ibid., 56.
40. Ibid., 55–56.
41. "I call heaven and Earth to witness against you today that I have set before you life and death, blessings and curses. Choose life so that you and your descendants may live ... " (Deut. 30:19).
42. Lynch, *Images of Hope*, 79–80.
43. Ibid., 80. He lists here some of those he has in mind: " ... the severely neurotic, the pervert, the addict, the homosexual.... "
44. Ibid., 80.
45. Ibid., 105.
46. "There is, after all, nothing wrong with dying according to a purely human mode in all its weakness and simplicity," ibid., 108.
47. Ibid., 109.
48. Ibid., 113.
49. Ibid., 112.
50. Ibid., 116–18. The allusion is to Dante, *Purgatorio*, Canto XXVII.
51. Ibid., 117.
52. For allusion to the nail, see Simone Weil, "The Love of God and Affliction," 134–35: "Extreme affliction, which means physical pain, distress of soul, and social degradation, all at the same time, is a nail whose point is applied at the very center of the soul, whose head is all necessity spreading throughout space and time.... In this marvelous dimension, the soul, without leaving the place and the instant where the body to which it is united is situated, can cross the totality of space and time and come into the very presence of God."
53. Miller, *The Way of Suffering*, 40.
54. Ibid., 146.
55. Ibid., 71.
56. Ibid., 49.
57. Ibid., 69.
58. Ibid., 41–42.
59. John of the Cross, *The Dark Night* in *Collected Works of St. John of the Cross*, trans. Kieran Cavanaugh and Otilio Rodriguez (Washington: ICS, 1979), 363–64.
60. See Lynch, *Images of Hope*, 81–88. See also Rahner, "Following the Crucified," *Theological Investigations*, 18:164.

Chapter 3: Searching for God

1. "O, in childhood, God ... " *The Unknown Rilke: Expanded Edition*, trans. Franz Wright (Oberlin, OH: Oberlin College Press, 1990), 109–10.
2. For key passages in *The Imitation of Christ* that speak of the cross, see Book II, Sections 11–13, in *The Imitation of Christ in Four Books by Thomas à Kempis*, trans. Joseph N. Tylenda (Wilmington, DE: Michael Glazier, 1984), 100. See also 97–105. For a critical approach to the authorship and scriptural

and theological sources at work in this text, see Kenneth M. Becker, *From the Treasure-House of Scripture: An Analysis of Scriptural Sources in "De Imitatione Christi"* (Turnhout, Belgium: Brepols, 2000), 15–49.

3. See Gustavo Gutiérrez, *A Theology of Liberation: History, Politics, and Salvation*, rev. ed. (Maryknoll, NY: Orbis, 1988), xx.

4. Jürgen Moltmann, *The Crucified God*, 276.

5. Ibid., 277.

6. Elie Wiesel, "Night," in *The Night Trilogy* (New York: Noonday Press, 1985), 71–72.

7. Moltmann, *The Crucified God*, 277–78

8. Ibid., 274.

9. Jon Sobrino, *Jesus the Liberator: A Historical-Theological View*, trans. Paul Burns and Francis McDonagh (Maryknoll, NY: Orbis, 1993), 238–39.

10. Ibid., 238.

11. Ibid., 240.

12. Ibid., 252.

13. Ibid., 252.

14. Dorothee Sölle, *Suffering* (Philadelphia: Fortress, 1975), 61–64.

15. Ibid., 64.

16. Ibid., 65–86.

17. Ibid., 85.

18. Ibid., 17.

19. Ibid., 24.

20. Ibid., 26.

21. Simone Weil in *Intimations of Christianity among the Greeks*, ed. and trans. by Elisabeth Chase Geissbuhler (London: Routledge and Kegan Paul, 1957), 24–26. Also translated by Mary McCarthy as *The Iliad: or, the Poem of Force* (Wallingford, PA: Pendle Hill, 1956), 3–5.

22. Weil, "The Love of God and Affliction," 133.

23. Ibid., 135.

24. Sölle, *Suffering*, 67.

25. Ibid., 75.

26. Gutiérrez, *God-Talk and the Suffering of the Innocent*, trans. Matthew J. O'Connell (Maryknoll, NY: Orbis, 1993), 101.

27. Sölle, *Suffering*, 14.

28. Ibid., 14.

29. Ibid., 24.

30. Ibid., 26.

31. Ibid., 32. On Abraham's sacrifice of Isaac, see James Alison, *Raising Abel: The Recovery of Eschatological Imagination* (New York: Crossroad, 1966), 45.

32. Sölle, *Suffering*, 22.

33. Ibid., 67.

34. Weil, "The Love of God and Affliction," 123–24.

35. Ibid., 125. James Alison speaks of the "random" selection of Jesus as victim, when his crucifixion is viewed within the mechanisms of violence that

led to the cross. He is dependent here on the theory of René Girard. See *Faith beyond Resentment: Fragments Catholic and Gay* (New York: Crossroad, 2001), esp. 152.

36. Sölle, *Suffering*, 75.

37. Metz, *A Passion for God*, 118. He adds: "Rahner resists any attempt on the part of theology to reconcile itself with God behind the back of the history of human suffering. He knows how such 'reconciliations' have led to the moral rebellion of human beings against God and have in this way turned out to be one of the roots, perhaps *the* root of modern atheism."

38. Sölle, *Suffering*, 163.

39. Ibid., 81–85.

40. Ibid., 86.

41. Ibid., 78.

42. Ibid., 157.

43. Ibid., 165.

44. See John Thiel, *God, Evil, and Innocent Suffering: A Theological Reflection* (New York: Crossroad, 2000). See also Terrence Tilley, *Evils of Theodicy* (Washington, DC: Georgetown, 1991).

45. John Hick, *Evil and the God of Love* (Norfolk, England: Collins/Fontana, 1968) 5. Kristiaan Depoortere traces the issue back to the fourth century, where Lactantius takes up the argument of Epicurus that an opposition exists between the power and the goodness of God (the gods). See *A Different God: A Christian View of Suffering* (Louvain, Belgium: Peeters Press, 1995), 49–50.

46. In addition to Thiel and Tilley, among the most trenchant criticisms have come from Kenneth Surin, *Theology and the Problem of Evil* (Oxford: Blackwell, 1986).

47. Thiel, *God, Evil, and Innocent Suffering*, 56.

48. Ibid., 58.

49. For a view of Jesus as the victim whose violent death breaks through the structures of victimization and sacrifice, see René Girard, *I See Satan Fall Like Lightning*, Trans. James G. Williams (Maryknoll, NY: Orbis, 2002).

50. Thiel, *God, Evil and Innocent Suffering*, 59.

51. Schillebeeckx, *Christ*, 730.

52. Thiel, *God, Evil and Innocent Suffering*, 59.

53. Anne E. Patrick, "Is Theodicy an Evil? Response to *The Evils of Theodicy* by Terrence W. Tilley," in *CTSA Proceedings* 5 (1995): 202. See Tilley, *Evils of Theodicy*, esp. 247–51, where he argues for counteracting the discourses of theodicy because they perpetuate the power of evil in the world.

54. Tracy, "Evil, Suffering, and Hope," 16–17.

55. John Hickey Wright, "Providence," *New Dictionary of Catholic Theology* (Collegeville, MN: Liturgical Press, 1988) 818.

56. Maritain, *God and the Permission of Evil*, trans. Joseph W. Evans (Milwaukee: Bruce, 1966) 1n (italics in original).

57. Rahner, *Theological Investigations* 19:194–208.

58. Rahner, "Why Does God Allow Us to Suffer?" *Theological Investigations* 19:196. For the German, see "Warum läßt Gott uns leiden?" in *Schriften zür Theologie*, Band XIV (Zürich: Benziger Verlag, 1980), 450–66 at 450. In Maritain's position, God is implicated, albeit indirectly. Rahner's "God allows" tried to steer a course around this conclusion because the lines between physical and metaphysical causality are so tenuously drawn.

59. Rahner, "Why Does God Allow Us to Suffer?" 195–96.

60. Ibid., 195.

61. Ibid., 196.

62. For Rahner's thorough treatment of the incomprehensibility of God, see "The Human Question of Meaning in Face of the Absolute Mystery of God," *Theological Investigations* 18:89–104. In this essay Rahner argues that any discussion of the divine freedom that abstracts from the freedom of God's self-communication in grace, which is always greater than human freedom, will result in an idol designed to fit human needs and expectations of God, and mere human designs of meaning.

63. Rahner, "Why Does God Allow Us to Suffer?," 206.

64. Rahner, "Following the Crucified," *Theological Investigations* 18:164.

Chapter 4: The Cross as Locus of the Divine Empathy

1. Nikos Kazantzakis, *Saint Francis*, trans. P. A. Bien (New York: Simon and Schuster, 1962) 90–96. Kazantzakis takes his inspiration from the *Legenda* of Bonaventure. For a discussion of this episode as foundational to Francis's vocation, and pivotal to his embrace of the cross, see Ephrem Longré, *François d'Assise et son expérience spirituelle* (Paris: Beauchesne, 1966), 16–18. The entire scene is rendered with near mystical power in Messiaen's opera *Saint François d'Assise*, where the opening lines, sung by Leo, are "J'ai peur sur la route."

2. Miller, *The Way of Suffering*, 175.

3. Paul Farmer and Arthur Leinman, "AIDS as Human Suffering," in *Living with AIDS*, ed. Stephen R. Graubard (Cambridge: MIT Press, 1990), 355. For more comparisons of AIDS with other new forms of disease, see Mirko D. Grmek, *History of AIDS: Emergence and Origin of a Modern Pandemic*, trans. Russell C. Maulitz and Jacalyn Duffin (Princeton: Princeton University Press, 1990) 101–9. For comparisons with syphilis, cholera, and polio, and reactions to epidemics in general, see Charles E. Rosenberg, "What Is an Epidemic? AIDS in Historical Perspective," in *Living with AIDS*, 1–17.

4. For an excellent presentation of the issues for theological ethics raised by AIDS, especially in relation to strategies for preventing the disease, see James F. Keenan, ed., *Catholic Ethicists on HIV/AIDS Prevention* (New York: Continuum, 2000).

5. For correspondences between Rahner's thought and that of Lynch, see William Dych, "Moving on to Fresh Horizons: The Discoveries of Karl Rahner and William Lynch," *Catholic Mind* 77 (1979): 9–19.

6. "Optimism, Pessimism and Religious Faith," in *The Essential Reinhold Niebuhr: Selected Essays and Addresses*, ed. Robert McAfee Brown (New Haven:

Yale University Press, 1986), 16. He concludes: "Let man stand at any point in history, even in a society which has realized his present dreams of justice, and if he surveys the human problem profoundly he will see that every perfection which has achieved points beyond itself to a greater perfection, and that this greater perfection throws light upon his sins and imperfections."

7. However, it must be said that for Niebuhr, the power of the cross resides primarily in its power as an ethical norm, demonstrating that the highest form of mutual love comes of sacrificial love. See *The Nature and Destiny of Man: A Christian Interpretation*, One Volume Edition of the Gifford Lectures (New York: Scribner's Sons, 1941), 2:69–70. While this underscoring of the ethical significance of the cross is certainly valid, we wish to emphasize here the fact that the cross also stands for the places where love meets the real, enters into reality, and redeems it.

8. Rahner, "Christian Pessimism," *Theological Investigations* 22:55–162 at 160.

9. Rahner, *On Prayer*, trans. of *Von der Not und dem Segen des Gebetes* (Collegeville, MN: Liturgical Press, 1993), 11.

10. Rahner, "Christian Pessimism," 155–62.

11. Rahner, "Utopia and Reality: The Shape of Christian Existence Caught between the Ideal and the Real," *Theological Investigations* 22:35.

12. See Martin Heidegger's "Memorial Address" in *Discourse on Thinking* [*Gelassenheit*], trans. John M. Anderson and E. Hans Freund (New York: Harper and Row, 1966) 46–47. For a discussion of the triumph of *techne* over *poiesis*, see George Steiner, *Martin Heidegger* (Chicago: University of Chicago, 1978). See also Paul G. Crowley, "Technology, Truth and Language: The Crisis of Theological Discourse," *Heythrop Journal* 32 (1991): 323–39.

13. Rahner, *Foundations of Christian Faith*, 403.

14. Niebuhr, "Optimism, Pessimism, and Religious Faith," 17.

15. Rahner, *Foundations of Christian Faith*, 402.

16. Ibid., 403.

17. Ibid., 110.

18. Ibid., 402.

19. Ibid., 107.

20. Ibid., 109.

21. Ibid., 109.

22. Ibid., 109.

23. See Bernard of Clairvaux, *On Loving God*, trans. Jean Leclercq and Henri Rochais, with analytical commentary by Emero Stiegman (Kalamazoo, MI: Cistercian, 1995) 36.

24. Rahner, *Foundations of Christian Faith*, 109.

25. Metz, *A Passion for God*, 117–19. Metz is quoting Rahner as in *Karl Rahner in Dialogue: Conversations and Interviews, 1965–1982* (New York: Crossroad, 1986), 126f.

26. Rahner, "Jesus Christ as the Meaning of Life," *The Love of Jesus and the Love of Neighbor*, trans. Robert Barr (New York: Crossroad, 1983), 59. Thus,

for Rahner, it would be more proper to speak in a Thomistic sense of Jesus as the "instrument of the divine" (*instrumentum divinitatis*). Thomas laid the groundwork for understanding Jesus in his human autonomy, and the uniqueness of his human experience, as the singular and unique locus of freedom for the exercise of God's saving work. See Paul G. Crowley, "*Instrumentum Divinitatis* in Thomas Aquinas: Recovering the Divinity of Christ," *Theological Studies* 52 (1991): 451–75.

27. Michael J. Dodds, "Thomas Aquinas, Human Suffering, and the Unchanging God of Love," *Theological Studies* 52 (1991): 330–44 at 339.

28. To my knowledge, this expression is the coinage of Gerald Vann, in *The Pain of Christ and the Sorrow of God* (Oxford: Blackfriars, 1949).

29. Ibid., 66–67.

30. See Rahner, *On the Theology of Death* (New York: Herder and Herder, 1961), 65, and "Following the Crucified," *Theological Investigations*, 18:166.

31. See Howard Gray, SJ, "Integrating Human Needs in Religious Formation," *Review for Religious* 53 (1994): 107–19 at 112, where he elaborates upon the experience of the Samaritan in Luke's account in a way that parallels the example of Francis: "The Samaritan 'saw' the reality before him, not his fear or his prejudice but a human being who had everything taken from him. If we are to be genuinely human, we need to see, to be able to let reality become part of our life, form our vision, catch our attention. Prayer, reflection, awareness, mutuality — the ability to be reverent and accepting — are radical human needs...."

32. See Miller, *The Way of Suffering*, 175.

Chapter 5: The Other Side of the Tapestry

1. Jacques Maritain to Julien Green, *The Story of Two Souls: The Correspondence of Jacques Maritain and Julien Green*, ed. Henry Bars and Eric Jourdan, trans. Bernard Doering (New York: Fordham University Press, 1988). Letter No. 29, June 1927, 65. [Hereinafter "Maritain and Green"].

2. In this chapter I use the terms "homosexual" and "gay" interchangeably as descriptors of an orientation.

3. No. 2358, *Catechism of the Catholic Church* (Collegeville, MN: Liturgical Press, 1994), 566. N.B.: The text was later changed to read: "The number of men and women who have deep-seated homosexual tendencies is not negligible. This inclination, which is objectively disordered, constitutes for most of them a trial."

4. "Am Kreuz der Sexualität: Ein Leben zwischen Katholizismus and Homosexualität," *Die Tageszeitung* (Berlin) August 19, 1998.

5. Maritain and Green, Letter No. 28, June 1927, 64.

6. Maritain and Green, Letter No. 31, June 29, 1927, 67.

7. Maritain and Green, Letter No. 29, June 1927, 65.

8. The reference is to Maritain's own marital arrangement with his wife, Raïssa.

9. See Letter No. 107, May 22, 1955, 138. On the other hand, Jean Cocteau was to say: "Max dreamed of chastity, and he was always punishing himself

because he could never attain it." As reported by Neal Oxenhandler in *Looking for Heroes in Postwar France: Albert Camus, Max Jacob, Simone Weil* (Dartmouth: University Press of New England, 1996), 146.

10. See Jacques Maritain, "Love and Friendship," *Notebooks*, trans. Joseph W. Evans (Albany, NY: Magi Books, 1984), 219–57, and esp. 222–25.

11. "Letter to All Catholic Bishops on the Pastoral Care of Homosexual Persons" (*Homosexualitatis Problema*), *Origins* 16, no. 22 (November 13, 1986): 379–82.

12. English Translation: "The Christian Meaning of Human Suffering," *Origins* 13, no. 37 (February 23, 1984): 609–24, at 618.

13. It should be noted that self-sacrifice in the form of sexual abstinence, though not necessarily in the name of the cross, is also recommended to other Catholics, notably the divorced and remarried. In the apostolic exhortation *Familiaris Consortio*, Pope John Paul II states (quoting himself at the end of this passage): "Reconciliation in the sacrament of Penance which would open the way to the Eucharist, can only be granted to those who, repenting of having broken the sign of the Covenant and of fidelity to Christ, are sincerely ready to undertake a way of life that is no longer in contradiction to the indissolubility of marriage. This means, in practice, that when, for serious reasons, such as for example the children's upbringing, a man and a woman cannot satisfy the obligation to separate, they 'take on themselves the duty to live in complete continence, that is, by abstinence from the acts proper to married couples.'" *Familiaris Consortio*, no. 84. ET: "The Apostolic Exhortation on the Family," *Origins* 11, no. 28–29 (December 24, 1981), 437–68 at 465.

14. See *Catechism of the Catholic Church*, no. 2359: "Homosexual persons are called to chastity. By the virtues of self-mastery that teach them inner freedom, at times by the support of disinterested friendship, by prayer and sacramental grace, they can and should gradually and resolutely approach Christian perfection." This teaching seems to recognize that "perfection" is not necessarily attained easily or through one single spiritual act or decision.

15. Matt. 10:39: "Those who find their life will lose it, and those who lose their life for my sake will find it." Cf. Mark 8:34; Luke 9:24; Luke 17:33; John 12:25.

16. Stephen J. Pope, "The Magisterium's Arguments against 'Same-Sex Marriage': An Ethical Analysis and Critique," *Theological Studies* 65 (2004): 552.

17. Ibid., 550.

18. Michele Dillon, *Catholic Identity: Balancing Reason, Faith, and Power* (Cambridge: Cambridge University Press, 1999), 115–63.

19. Donald Cozzens, *Sacred Silence: Denial and the Crisis in the Church* (Collegeville, MN: Liturgical Press, 2002), 135–36. This topic is treated extensively by Mark D. Jordan in the second part of *The Silence of Sodom: Homosexuality in Modern Catholicism* (Chicago: University of Chicago Press, 2000), 83–208.

20. Eugene Kennedy, *The Unhealed Wound: The Church and Human Sexuality* (New York: St. Martin's Griffin, 2001), 39.

21. Pope, "The Magisterium's Arguments against 'Same-Sex Marriage,'" 550–52.

22. Paul Ricoeur, "Wonder, Eroticism, and Enigma," as edited in *Sexuality and the Sacred: Sources for Theological Reflection*, ed. James B. Nelson and Sandra P. Longfellow (Louisville: Westminster/John Knox Press, 1994), 80–84.

23. Ibid., 80.

24. Ibid., 83.

25. Ibid., 84.

26. Ibid.

27. Sarah Coakley, "Living into the Mystery of the Holy Trinity: Trinity, Prayer and Sexuality," *Anglican Theological Review* 80 (1998): 223–32 at 230. But she also warns, "no language of *eros* is safe from possible nefarious application . . ." (231).

28. Rahner, *Foundations of Christian Faith*, 404. For a sampling of the many places where such an embrace is clearly laid out, see "Following the Crucified," *Theological Investigations* 18:157–70, and "Lent," in *The Eternal Year*, trans. John Shea (Baltimore: Helicon, 1964), 65–72.

29. *Foundations of Christian Faith*, 404.

30. Rahner asks, "Can we say of ourselves that we carry the mark of Christ's death on us as the sign of our election?" *Spiritual Exercises*, trans. Kenneth Baker (New York: Herder and Herder, 1965), 243.

31. Rahner, *Spiritual Exercises*, 241.

32. "The Theological Concept of Concupiscencia," *Theological Investigations* 1:382.

33. Rahner, *Grace in Freedom*, trans. Hilda Graef (New York: Herder and Herder, 1969), 120.

34. Rahner, "Gratitude for the Cross," trans. Daniel Donovan, as in *The Content of Faith: The Best of Karl Rahner's Theological Writings*, ed. Karl Lehmann and Albert Raffelt (New York: Crossroad, 1992), 309.

35. Rahner, *Grace in Freedom*, 120.

36. Rahner, "Reflections on the Theology of Renunciation," *Theological Investigations* 3:50.

37. Rahner, *Spiritual Exercises*, 242–43.

38. Rahner, "Reflections on a Theology of Renunciation," 54. Italics in original.

39. Ibid., 55.

40. Rahner, "The Eucharist and Suffering," *Theological Investigations* 3:161–70.

41. Ibid., 170.

42. Ibid., 167–68. Emphasis added.

Chapter 6: A Cross That Leads to Hope

1. Jon Sobrino, *Christ the Liberator: A View from the Victims*, trans. Paul Burns (Maryknoll, NY: Orbis, 2001), 49.

2. Francesco Calvo, *Church of St. Ignatius Rome* (Bologna: Officine grafiche Poligrafici il Resto del Carlino, 1968), 27.

3. My approach to the Pozzo painting does not take into account the standard reading of it as "a dialectic between the name of Jesus, chosen for the Society by the saint, and 'ignis,' fire, a pun on the name of Ignatius." "Depicted at the center of the field, high above the four parts of the earth, the saint is struck by rays of light emanating from Christ's wounded side.... From the heart of Ignatius, as from a mirror, light issues to the four corners of the earth. The converting power of this light or flame is mediated by the Jesuit saints who travelled to the four continents as missionaries. The sending of the missionaries and the spreading of fire on earth are taken from the gospel and communion antiphons, respectively, for Ignatius' mass proper" (Yvonne Levy, untitled essay in *Saint, Site and Sacred Strategy: Ignatius, Rome and Jesuit Urbanism*, ed. Thomas M. Lucas [Rome: Biblioteca Apostolica Vaticana, 1990], 216. 216). Calvo writes that Pozzo confirms the connection between the name of Ignatius and the motto *Ignem veni mettere in terram.* "Pozzo himself supplies a precise explanation of the significance of his fresco: 'Jesus illumines the heart of St. Ignatius with a ray of light, which is then transmitted by the Saint to the furthermost corners of the four quarters of the earth, which I have represented with their symbols in the four sections of the vault.' Referring to the missionaries of the Society of Jesus he writes: 'The first of these indefatigable workers is St. Francis Xavier, the Apostle of the Indies, who is seen leading a vast crowd of Eastern converts towards Heaven. The same kind of scene i[s] depicted with other members of the Society of Jesus in Europe, Africa and America'" (Calvo, 29).

4. Ignatius, "Autobiography," no. 96, as in *St. Ignatius' Own Story: As told to Luis Gonzalez de Camara, with a Sampling of His Letters*, trans. William J. Young (Chicago: Loyola University Press, 1980), 66–67.

5. See Joseph de Guibert, *The Jesuits: Their Spiritual Doctrine and Practice — A Historical Study*, trans. William J. Young (Chicago: Institute of Jesuit Sources, 1964), 534–39. The rich biblical foundations of the Exercises, and their rendering as a kind of pedagogy of Scripture is discussed by Giles Cusson, *Pédagogie de l'expérience personnelle: Bible et Exercices* (Paris: Desclée de Brouwer, 1968).

6. Jean Daniélou, "The Ignatian Vision of the Universe and of Man," *Cross Currents* 4 (1954): 358.

7. *Sp Exx* [53]: "*Colloquy:* Imagining Christ our Lord present and placed on the cross, let me make a colloquy, how from Creator He is come to making Himself man, and from life eternal is come to temporal death, and so to die for my sins. Likewise, looking at myself, what I have done for Christ, what I am doing for Christ, what I ought to do for Christ. And so, seeing Him such, and so nailed on the cross, to go over that which will present itself." Quotations from the Spiritual Exercises are abbreviated *Sp Exx*, followed in brackets by the standard paragraph number. All quotations are from the Mullan translation, which appears in David Fleming, *Draw Me Into Your Friendship, The Spiritual Exercises: A Literal Translation And a Contemporary Reading* (St. Louis: Institute of Jesuit Sources, 1996).

8. *Sp Exx* [204–9].

9. Rahner, "Christian Pessimism," 160–61.

10. Ibid.

11. Leo O'Donovan, "A Journey into Time: The Legacy of Karl Rahner's Last Years," *Theological Studies* 46 (1985): 89–104 at 642.

12. Rahner, "Following the Crucified," 169–70.

13. Rahner, *On the Theology of Death*, 48; cf. Leo O'Donovan, "Karl Rahner, S.J. (1904–1984) In Memoriam," *Cross Currents* 34 (1984): 211–12.

14. Rahner, "Christian Dying," *Theological Investigations* 18:245–47.

15. Weil, "The 'Iliad,' Poem of Might," 41.

16. Ibid., 54.

17. Rahner, *Foundations of Christian Faith*, 404. Italics added.

18. Rahner, *On the Theology of Death*, 64.

19. Ibid., 48–51, 58.

20. Rahner, *Foundations of Christian Faith*, 404.

21. Rahner, "Utopia and Reality: The Shape of Christian Existence Caught between the Ideal and the Real," *Theological Investigations* 22:142.

22. See Guy Gaucher, *The Passion of Thérèse of Lisieux, 4 April–30 September 1897* (New York: Crossroad, 1990), esp. 97–122, which describes her struggles with faith itself in the course of her illness.

23. *Sp Exx* [95].

24. *Sp Exx* [98].

25. *Sp Exx* [102].

26. *Sp Exx* [103].

27. *Sp Exx* [104].

28. *Sp Exx* [106].

29. Rahner, *Spiritual Exercises*, 147.

30. Rahner, "Jesus Christ as the Meaning of Life," in *The Love of Jesus and the Love of Neighbor*, trans. Robert Barr (New York: Crossroad, 1983), 56. Jerome Miller, in a less theological vein, sees in children the promise that can be realized in accepting our dying as a summons into a sacred mystery. See Miller, "Joy and Gravity: A Meditation on the Will to Live," *Second Opinion* 20 (1994): 57–69. " . . . [T]he promise of childhood, its potential for extravagant praise-giving, is fully realized only by the dying who give themselves unreservedly to life precisely by irrevocably relinquishing their hold on it. . . . Our own deaths may not be imminent. But it is not the imminence of death that makes the acceptance of it wise." (67)

31. Rahner, "Utopia and Reality," 142.

32. Rahner, "The Human Question of Meaning in Face of the Absolute Mystery of God," *Theological Investigations* 18:94.

33. Rahner, "Christian Pessimism," 157.

34. Ibid., 161.

35. Rahner, *The Eternal Year*, trans. John Shea (Baltimore: Helicon Press, 1964), 68–69.

36. *Sp Exx* [196].

37. As in Jon Sobrino, *Christ the Liberator: A View from the Victims,* trans. Paul Burns (Maryknoll, NY: Orbis, 2001), 12.

38. See John O'Malley, "Early Jesuit Spirituality," in *Christian Spirituality: Post-Reformation and Modern,* ed. Louis Dupré and Don E. Saliers (New York: Crossroad, 1989), 18.

39. Philip Endean, "The Ignatian Prayer of the Senses," *Heythrop Journal* 31 (1990): 410.

40. Sobrino, *Spirituality of Liberation: Toward Political Holiness,* trans. Robert R. Barr (Maryknoll, NY: Orbis, 1989), esp. ix–x and "The Importance of the Spiritual Life Today," 1–10.

41. Sobrino, *Christ the Liberator,* 3–4. Six Jesuits at the Universidad Centroamericana José Simeón Cañas in San Salvador, who stood as voices for social justice in El Salvador, were brutally slain on the night of November 16, 1989, by members of the Salvadoran armed forces. They were joined in martyrdom by their housekeeper and her daughter. This event had a profound effect on Sobrino and his theology. Sobrino, who was a member of the community, happened to be out of the country on the night of the killings. He spent the following six months in residence at Santa Clara University writing about the tragedy.

42. Ibid., 4.

43. Here we encounter the "real" in yet a more concrete sense than we have yet encountered, that developed by the Spanish philosopher Xavier Zubiri, who greatly influenced both Ellacuría and Sobrino. See Sobrino, *Jesus the Liberator,* 34.

44. See Gustavo Gutiérrez, "Expanding the View," in *A Theology of Liberation,* 12.

45. Sobrino, "Presuppositions and Foundations of Spirituality," in *Spirituality of Liberation,* 18.

46. Sobrino, "The Spirituality of Persecution and Martyrdom," in *Spirituality of Liberation,* 87–102.

47. Sobrino, "Presuppositions and Foundations of Spirituality," 19.

48. Ibid., 20–21.

Afterword

1. Rainer Maria Rilke, "Pieta," in Franz Wright, trans., *The Unknown Rilke: Expanded Edition* (Oberlin, OH: Oberlin College Press, 1990), 75.

Bibliography

Adams, Marilyn McCord. *Horrendous Evils and the Goodness of God.* Ithaca, NY: Cornell University Press, 1999.

Barnes, Michael. "Demythologization in the Theology of Karl Rahner." *Theological Studies* 55 (1994): 24–45.

Bednar, Gerald J. *Faith as Imagination: The Contribution of William F. Lynch, S.J.* Kansas City, MO: Sheed and Ward, 1966.

Berguerie, Pantxika. *The Unterlinden Museum.* Colmar, France: Unterlinden Museum, 1999.

Bernard of Clairvaux. *On Loving God.* Trans. Jean Leclercq and Henri Rochais. Kalamazoo, MI: Cistercian Publications, 1995.

———. *The Works of Bernard of Clairvaux.* Vol. 3. Trans. Kilian Walsh. Kalamazoo, MI: Cistercian Publications, 1976.

Brown, Robert McAfee, ed. *The Essential Reinhold Niebuhr: Selected Essays and Addresses.* New Haven: Yale University Press, 1986.

Calvo, Francesco. *Church of St. Ignatius Rome.* Bologna: Officine grafiche Poligrafici il Resto del Carlino, 1968.

Coakley, Sarah. "Living into the Mystery of the Holy Trinity: Trinity, Prayer and Sexuality." *Anglican Theological Review* 80 (1998): 223–32.

Congregation for the Doctrine of the Faith. *Catechism of the Catholic Church.* Rev. edition. Collegeville, MN: Liturgical Press, 1994.

———. "Letter to All Catholic Bishops on the Pastoral Care of Homosexual Persons" ("*Homosexualitatis Problema*"). *Origins* 16. no. 22 (November 13, 1986): 379–82.

Cozzens, Donald. *Sacred Silence: Denial and the Crisis in the Church.* Collegeville, MN: Liturgical Press, 2002.

de Guibert, Joseph. *The Jesuits: Their Spiritual Doctrine and Practice — A Historical Study.* Trans. William J. Young. Chicago: Institute of Jesuit Sources, 1964.

Daniélou, Jean. "The Ignatian Vision of the Universe and of Man." *Cross Currents* 4 (1954): 357–66.

Dillon, Michele. *Catholic Identity: Balancing Reason, Faith, and Power.* Cambridge: Cambridge University Press, 1999.

Dodds, Michael J. "Thomas Aquinas, Human Suffering, and the Unchanging God of Love." *Theological Studies* 52 (1991): 330–44.

Dych, William. "Moving on to Fresh Horizons: The Discoveries of Karl Rahner and William Lynch." *Catholic Mind* 77 (1979): 9–19.

Endean, Philip. "The Ignatian Prayer of the Senses." *Heythrop Journal* 31 (1990): 3910–418.

Farmer, Paul, and Arthur Leinman. "AIDS as Human Suffering." In *Living with AIDS*. Ed. Stephen R. Graubard. Cambridge: MIT, 1990.

Gadamer, Hans Georg. *The Enigma of Health: The Art of Healing in a Scientific Age*. Trans Jason Gaiger and Nicholas Walker. Stanford: Stanford University Press, 1966.

Gilman, Sander L. *Disease and Representation: Images of Illness from Madness to AIDS*. Ithaca, NY: Cornell University Press, 1988.

Girard, René. *I See Satan Fall Like Lightning*. Maryknoll, NY: Orbis, 2002.

Glover, Jonathan. *Humanity: A Moral History of the Twentieth Century*. New Haven: Yale University Press, 1999.

Gray, Howard. "Integrating Human Needs in Religious Formation." *Review for Religious* 53 (1994): 107–19.

Gutiérrez, Gustavo. *A Theology of Liberation: History, Politics, and Salvation*. Rev. ed. Maryknoll, NY: Orbis, 1988.

———. *God-Talk and the Suffering of the Innocent*. Trans. Matthew J. O'Connell. Maryknoll, NY: Orbis, 1993.

Haight, Roger. *Jesus: Symbol of God*. Maryknoll: NY: Orbis, 1999.

Heidegger, Martin. *Discourse on Thinking*. Trans. John M. Anderson and E. Hans Freund. New York: Harper and Row, 1966.

Hick, John. *Evil and the God of Love*. Norfolk, England: Collins/Fontana, 1968.

Ignatius of Loyola, St. "Autobiography," as in *St. Ignatius' Own Story: As Told to Luis Gonzalez de Camara, with a Sampling of his Letters*. Trans. William J. Young. Chicago: Loyola University Press, 1980.

———. "Spiritual Exercises," as in *Draw Me into Your Friendship, The Spiritual Exercises: A Literal Translation And a Contemporary Reading*. Ed. David Fleming. St. Louis: Institute of Jesuit Sources, 1996.

"The Imitation of Christ." *The Imitation of Christ in Four Books by Thomas à Kempis*. Trans. Joseph N. Tylenda. Wilmington, DE: Michael Glazier, 1984.

John of the Cross, St. *The Dark Night*, in *Collected Works of St. John of the Cross*. Trans. Kieran Cavanaugh and Otilio Rodriguez. Washington, DC: ICS, 1979.

John Paul II, Pope. "The Christian Meaning of Human Suffering" (*Salvifici Doloris*). Encyclical. *Origins* 13, no. 37 (February 23, 1984): 609–24.

Kazantzakis, Nikos. *Saint Francis*. Trans. P. A. Bien. New York: Simon and Schuster, 1962.

Keenan, James F., ed. *Catholic Ethicists on HIV/AIDS Prevention*. New York: Continuum, 2000.

Kennedy, Eugene. *The Unhealed Wound: The Church and Human Sexuality*. New York: St. Martin's Griffin, 2001.

Lewis, C. S. *A Grief Observed*. London: Faber and Faber, 1961.

Lynch, William. *Images of Hope: Imagination as Healer of the Hopeless*. Notre Dame: University of Notre Dame Press, 1965.

————. "The Imagination of the Drama." *Review of Existential Psychology and Psychiatry* 14 (1975–76): 1–10.

————. "Theology and the Imagination." *Thought* 29 (1954): 61–86.

————. "Theology and the Imagination II: The Evocative Symbol." *Thought* 29 (1954): 529–54.

————. "Theology and the Imagination III: The Problem of Comedy." *Thought* 30 (1955): 18–36.

Maritain, Jacques. *God and the Permission of Evil.* Trans. Joseph W. Evans. Milwaukee: Bruce, 1966.

————. *Notebooks.* Trans. Joseph W. Evans. Albany, NY: Magi Books, 1984.

————, and Julien Green. *The Story of Two Souls: The Correspondence of Jacques Maritain and Julien Green.* Ed. Henry Bars and Eric Jourdan. Trans. Bernard Doering. New York: Fordham University Press, 1988.

Marshall, Dennis. "Into the Inescapable Darkness: Karl Rahner's Theology of Redemptive Suffering." Diss. Duquesne University, 1997.

Messiaen, Olivier. *Saint François d'Assise.* Opera and libretto (445 176-2). Deutsche Grammaphon, 1999.

Metz, Johannes. *A Passion for God: The Mystical-Political Dimension of Christianity.* Trans. J. Matthew Ashley. New York: Paulist, 1998.

Miller, Jerome. *The Way of Suffering: A Geography of Crisis.* Washington, DC: Georgetown University Press, 1988.

Moltmann, Jürgen. *The Crucified God: The Cross of Christ as the Foundation and Criticism of Christian Theology.* Trans. R. A. Wilson and John Bowden. Minneapolis: Fortress Press, 1993.

O'Donovan, Leo. "A Journey into Time: The Legacy of Karl Rahner's Last Years." *Theological Studies* 46 (1985): 89–104.

O'Malley, John. "Early Jesuit Spirituality." In *Christian Spirituality: Post-Reformation and Modern.* Ed. Louis Dupré and Don E. Saliers. New York: Crossroad, 1989.

Patrick, Anne. "Is Theodicy an Evil? Response to The Evils of Theodicy by Terrence W. Tilley." *Proceedings of the Catholic Theological Society of America* 50 (1995): 201–4.

Pétrement, Simone. *Simone Weil: A Life.* Trans. Raymond Rosenthal. New York: Pantheon, 1976.

Pope, Stephen J. "The Magisterium's Arguments against 'Same-Sex Marriage': An Ethical Analysis and Critique." *Theological Studies* 65 (2004): 530–65.

Rahner, Karl. "Christian Dying." *Theological Investigations* 18:226–56.

————. "Christian Pessimism." *Theological Investigations* 22:55–162.

————. *The Content of Faith: The Best of Karl Rahner's Theological Writings.* Ed. Karl Lehmann and Albert Raffelt. New York: Crossroad, 1992.

————. "The Eucharist and Suffering." *Theological Investigations* 3:161–70.

————. *The Eternal Year.* Trans. John Shea. Baltimore: Helicon, 1964.

————. "Following the Crucified." *Theological Investigations* 18:157–70.

————. *Foundations of Christian Faith.* Trans. William Dych. New York: Crossroad, 1998.

————. *Grace in Freedom.* Trans. Hilda Graef. New York: Herder and Herder, 1969.

————. "The Human Question of Meaning in the Face of the Absolute Mystery of God." *Theological Investigations* 18:89–104.

————. *The Love of Jesus and the Love of Neighbor.* Trans. Robert Barr. New York: Crossroad, 1983.

————. *On Prayer.* Trans. anon. Collegeville, MN: Liturgical Press, 1993.

————. "Reflections on the Theology of Renunciation." *Theological Investigations* 3:47–57.

————. *Spiritual Exercises.* Trans. Kenneth Baker. New York: Herder and Herder, 1965.

————. "The Theological Concept of Concupiscencia." *Theological Investigations* 1:347–82.

————. *On the Theology of Death.* New York: Herder and Herder, 1961.

————. "Utopia and Reality: The Shape of Christian Existence Caught between the Ideal and the Real." *Theological Investigations* 22:26–37.

————. "Why Does God Allow Us to Suffer?" *Theological Investigations* 19:204–8.

Ricoeur, Paul. "Wonder, Eroticism and Enigma." In *Sexuality and the Sacred: Sources for Theological Reflection.* Ed. James B. Nelson and Sandra P. Longfellow. Louisville: Westminster/John Knox Press, 1994.

Rilke, Rainer Maria. *The Unknown Rilke: Expanded Edition.* Trans. Franz Wright. Oberlin, OH: Oberlin College Press, 1990.

Scarry, Elaine. *The Body in Pain: The Making and Unmaking of the World.* New York: Oxford University Press, 1985.

Schillebeeckx, Edward. *Christ: The Experience of Jesus as Lord.* Trans. John Bowden. New York: Crossroad, 1989.

Schner, George. "The Appeal to Experience." *Theological Studies* 53 (1992): 40–59.

Smith, Jeffery. *Where the Roots Reach for Water: A Personal and Natural History of Melancholia.* New York: North Point Press, 1999.

Sobrino, John. *Jesus the Liberator: A Historical-Theological View.* Trans. Paul Burns and Francis McDonagh. Maryknoll, NY: Orbis, 1993.

————. *Christ the Liberator: A View from the Victims.* Trans. Paul Burns. Maryknoll, NY 2001.

————. *Spirituality of Liberation: Toward Political Holiness.* Trans. Robert R. Barr. Maryknoll, NY: Orbis, 1989.

————. *Where Is God? Earthquake, Terrorism, Barbarity, and Hope.* Trans. Margaret Wilde. Maryknoll, NY: Orbis, 2004.

Sölle, Dorothee. *Suffering.* Philadelphia: Fortress Press, 1975.

Sontag, Susan. *Illness as Metaphor and AIDS and Its Metaphors.* New York: Doubleday, 1990.

Thiel, John. *God, Evil and Innocent Suffering: A Theological Reflection.* New York: Crossroad, 2000.

Thomas Aquinas, St. *Summa Theologiae,* II-II, Biblioteca de Autores Cristianos. Vol. 3. Madrid, 1952.

Tilley, Terrence W. *Evils of Theodicy.* Washington, DC: Georgetown University Press, 1991.

Tracy, David. "Evil, Suffering, Hope: The Search for New Forms of Contemporary Theodicy." *Proceedings of the Catholic Theological Society of America* 50 (1995): 15–36.

Vann, Gerald. *The Pain of Christ and the Sorrow of God.* Oxford: Blackfriars, 1949.

von Balthasar, Hans Urs. *The Moment of Christian Witness.* Trans. Richard Beckley. Glen Rock, NJ: Newman, 1966.

Weil, Simone. "The 'Iliad,' Poem of Might." In *Intimations of Christianity among the Greeks.* Ed. and trans. Elisabeth Chase Geissbuhler. London: Routledge and Kegan Paul, 1957.

———. *Waiting for God.* Trans. Emma Craufurd. New York: Harper and Row, 1951.

Wiesel, Elie. *The Night Trilogy.* New York: Noonday Press, 1985.

Wright, John Hickey. "Providence." *New Dictionary of Catholic Theology.* Collegeville, MN: Liturgical Press, 1988.

Index

cross (*continued*)
  and sin, 133
  as symbol of hope, 56, 93, 127, 131,
    137–39
  as symbol of love, 74, 117–19

death
  and the cross, 118–19, 133
  and hope, 137–38
  Rahner on, 132–34, 137
  reality of, 132–34
  and suffering, 30–32
Dillon, Michele, 113
disease, 38, 82–83. *See also* illness
Dodds, Michael, 99

Ecclesiastes, 26
Ellacuría, Ignacio, 140
empathy
  Christian asceticism and, 122–23
  eschatology and, 142–43
  of God, 99–103, 122–24
  paschal mystery and, 123–24
Eros
  God and, 117
  sexuality and, 115–17
eroticism, 115–17
escapism, 11, 12, 45, 49, 54, 120
eschatology
  empathy and, 142–43
  Ignatian imagination and, 128,
    130–31, 139–43
  solidarity and, 127, 131, 142–43
Eucharist, counsel of the cross and,
  106, 109, 121–22
"Eucharist and Suffering, The"
  (Rahner), 121–22
Exodus, 76

Familiaris Consortio (John Paul II),
  160n13
1 Thessalonians, 122
Francis of Assisi, Saint, 33, 85–86,
  102–3, 144, 147

Gadamer, Hans-Georg, 34–35
Galatians, 108, 109
gay and lesbian Catholics, 15, 110–12
  suffering of, 112–14
*Glory (or Apotheosis) of St. Ignatius,
The* (Pozzo), 129–30, 141,
  142, 162n3
God
  absence/presence of, 37, 68–69,
    74–75, 138–39
  and AIDS, 88
  empathy of, 99–103
  and Eros, 117
  found in solidarity, 40, 69
  as Mystery, 84, 132
  presence in the cross, 68–69, 93,
    138–39
  suffering and,
    allowed by, 81–83
    Aquinas on, 80
    Augustine on, 80
    caused by, 70–73
    Leibniz on, 77, 80
    Maritain on, 80
    permitted by, 77, 80
    present in, 40, 68–69, 138–39,
      83–84, 98
    Rahner on, 81–84
    witnessed by, 78
"going through"
  reality, 54, 57–58, 95
  suffering, 45–46, 54, 57–58, 95
Green, Julien, 105–7
Grief Observed, A (Lewis), 31–32
Grünewald, Matthias
  Isenheim altarpiece, 44–46, 50, 52, 54,
    58
Gutiérrez, Gustavo, 72

Haight, Roger, 26
health, mystery of, 34–35
Hebrews, 11–12, 92, 109
Hick, John, 77
Holocaust, 25, 67–68, 79
Homosexualitatis problema, 107–9, 110